NEW FOREST

NATIONAL PARK

NEW FOREST
NATIONAL PARK

CLIVE CHATTERS
and
MIKE READ

HALSGROVE

First published in Great Britain in 2006

British Library Cataloguing-in-Publication Data
A CIP record for this title is available from the British Library

ISBN 1 84114 358 8
ISBN 978 1 84114 358 3

HALSGROVE
Halsgrove House
Lower Moor Way
Tiverton, Devon EX16 6SS
Tel: 01884 243242
Fax: 01884 243325
email: sales@halsgrove.com
website: www.halsgrove.com

Printed and bound by D'Auria Industrie Grafiche Spa, Italy

CONTENTS

NEW FOREST NATIONAL PARK

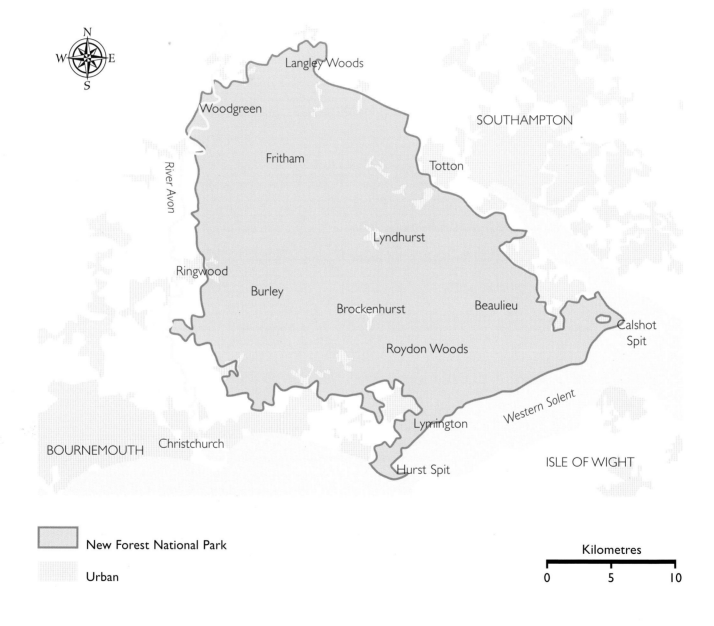

N W E S

Langley Woods

Woodgreen

SOUTHAMPTON

Fritham

River Avon

Totton

Lyndhurst

Ringwood

Burley

Brockenhurst

Beaulieu

Calshot Spit

Roydon Woods

Western Solent

Lymington

BOURNEMOUTH Christchurch

Hurst Spit

ISLE OF WIGHT

New Forest National Park

Urban

Kilometres

0   5   10

INTRODUCTION
AND ACKNOWLEDGEMENTS

The New Forest is a place where ancient traditions of land management support an intriguing landscape and way of life. The Forest is not a museum, a country park nor a nature reserve. The Forest is a real place where ordinary people choose to live out-of-the-ordinary lives and by doing so maintain one of Britain's richest and most diverse landscapes.

In March 2005 the New Forest was designated a National Park. In this book we look at what makes the National Park special and offer ideas so that readers can discover the New Forest for themselves.

In this book we have tried to cover the whole Forest within the National Park. We start by looking at the Open Forest where the ponies are free to roam. We then look at the coast and countryside of the National Park and conclude with thoughts on the future.

This is not intended to be a text book. There are already excellent reference books about the Forest. This is an introduction to the National Park. We have tried to give answers to the questions that are often asked by people who want to get to know the Forest better. We hope that this book will be an inspiration to readers to go on to find out more about the Forest.

We are particularly grateful for the help of Amanda Craig from English Nature, Jolyon Chesworth and Debbie King of Hampshire Wildlife Trust, Peter Frost the Amenity Verderer, Jonathan Gerrelli the Head Agister, Martin O'Neill of the New Forest National Park Authority, Richard Reeves at the Christopher Tower Library, Ann Sevier of Blissford, Sue Westwood the clerk to the Verderers and Simon Weymouth of the Forestry Commission. Many thanks also to Forestry Commission keepers, active and retired, particularly Maurice Holland, Martin Noble, Andy Page, Andy Shore and Ian Young.

DISCOVERING THE FOREST:
WHAT'S IN A NAME?

When getting to know the New Forest you meet words whose meanings may at first seem obscure or confusing. These words are not just for historians and scholars but form part of an everyday language for those who live and work in the Forest. As the language of the Forest is a living part of its culture and landscape, then understanding these words is important. The vocabulary of the Forest is one of the things which make it special.

The first and most important word to understand is that of 'Forest'. In our modern language forest is usually used to describe landscapes dominated by trees, but this use does not apply to the New Forest. The name New Forest arises from the heritage of forest law and dates back to at least 1079, shortly after the Norman conquest.

Historically, forests in England were areas of land where people not only had to obey the law of the land but they also had to obey forest law. In medieval England there were many forests, and the New Forest was not particularly special. Forest law sought to protect the King's right to use natural resources such as timber and venison. Forests could contain all sorts of landscapes, with farms and fields being included as well as open heaths, grasslands and woods.

Over the centuries, forest law became weaker and forests declined in importance. The last remnants of forest law were repealed by Parliament as late as 1971. For much of England the historic use of the word Forest is now limited to a name on a map. The management and culture of the New Forest is a direct descendant of the medieval Forest with its own law and administrative system.

Locally you hear people refer not to the New Forest but simply to 'the Forest' – as if it were the only one in the world.

Opposite: Ponies graze the Open Forest at Whitefield Moor.

THE OPEN FOREST

The picture postcard image of the National Park is a place of open spaces where New Forest ponies wander about. The places where Forest animals are free to roam is called the Open Forest.

The Open Forest includes many landscapes. The largest of these are the heaths, bogs and grazed woodlands. The Open Forest however also includes smaller, more intimate, landscapes. Forest villages often have their village greens in the Open Forest with grazing animals providing a picturesque addition to cottages and cricket pitches.

Forest animals graze along well hedged country lanes and into villages such as Beaulieu, Brockenhurst and Burley. Here animals may gather in the village streets, looking into the doorways of cottages and shops. The Open Forest lanes wind their way between fields and small woodlands. The lanes lead down to the coast near Lymington where cattle and ponies graze the shore and saltmarshes of the Solent.

Donkeys on the Open Forest at Burley.

Opposite: *The Lyndhurst Cricket Pitch by Bolton's Bench.*

By knowing the Open Forest well, it is possible to walk from any one place on the Open Forest to any other without ever crossing a fence. If a Forest pony really wanted to, it could roam from the banks of the River Avon near Woodgreen to the saltmarshes of the Boldre foreshore.

Why is the Open Forest Special?

There was a time when the New Forest was not particularly special. Places similar to the New Forest in the way land was owned and managed were once widespread across the lowlands of western Europe. The Open Forest is remarkable in that these things have not only survived on a large scale, but have also found a way to fit in with the modern world.

It is how people live and work in the landscape which is the heart of what makes the Open Forest special. The landscape and wildlife is the result of how the land has been owned and managed over centuries. The Open Forest is managed through a living tradition based on the ancient rights and responsibilities of commoning.

No where else in Britain is there such a complete heathland landscape as can be found in the Open Forest. Heathlands elsewhere have become fragments of their former selves. Heaths are far more than just a purple carpet of heather; they have woods, rivers, lawns, lanes and bogs all merging into one another. As well as the natural features within the Open Forest there are marks on the landscapes recording how people have lived in the Forest over thousands of years. The landscape is not frozen in time; each age has left its mark but still the sense of wildness is dominant.

Above: *Hampton Ridge.*

Right: *The Open Forest includes parts of the Solent foreshore.*

Opposite: *The rolling heathlands of the Open Forest at Stone Quarry Bottom near Godshill.*

The wildlife of the Open Forest is exceptional. The Open Forest is recognised as being one of the richest places for wildlife in Europe and one of the best wetlands in the world. The Open Forest has a great diversity of things which live there from the landscape scale right down to the fine detail on the bark of an individual tree, in a mucky puddle or under a square of turf.

As other parts of our countryside have become built over and more intensively farmed, the Open Forest has become special as a place for quiet enjoyment for millions of people. The Open Forest is by far the largest landscape open to the public in lowland England.

The Perambulation

…and thence as far as the bridge of Forthingebridge (Fordingbridge), and thence just as the river bank of the Avene (Avon) extends as far as Moletone (Breamore Mill), and thence just as far as the river bank of the Avene extends as far as Northchardeford (North Charford Farm)…

Extract from the perambulation of King Edward I in 1278

Breamore Mill: marking the boundary of the New Forest for over 700 years.

Over the centuries the land that makes up the Open Forest has changed. In modern times the legal limits of the Forest have been set by Acts of Parliament. In the centuries before reliable maps, the boundary of the Forest was recorded by people walking around the edge and writing down descriptions of the landmarks along the way. These boundaries are recorded in royal charters. The legal boundary of the Open Forest is known as the perambulation – quite literally a walk.

The most recent perambulation was mapped and defined by Act of Parliament in 1964. The 1964 perambulation reflected not only the historic Forest boundaries but also the practical need to build cattle grids across busy main roads to separate cars from livestock. This 1964 perambulation resulted in major losses to the Open Forest along its boundary with Southampton Water at Hythe. Forest animals were also fenced out from many miles of droves and village greens from the coast to Dorset and Wiltshire.

Over the years the purpose of the perambulation has changed. The early perambulations described the land subject to forest law and excluded many places that today we think of as classic New Forest landscapes. The modern perambulation includes all of the Open Forest as well as large areas of hedged countryside and the coast at Boldre. The modern perambulation includes an area of 37,907ha.

The amount of Open Forest within the perambulation is constantly changing. At present, just over half of the area within the perambulation is Open Forest. Recent years have seen the Open Forest grow in some places with the restoration of conifer plantations to heathland, and shrink in other areas, with the fencing of lanes leading down to the coast and the inclosure of grazed woodland such as at Irons Hill near Ashurst.

In the recent historic past the major changes in the area of Open Forest have come about because of enclosures and inclosures.

Inclosures and Enclosures

A map of the Forest shows places called inclosures. These are areas of land, usually forestry plantations, which have been fenced out of the Open Forest on Crown land to allow commercial crops of trees to be grown. Making and managing inclosures is closely controlled through Acts of Parliament.

The first Act of Parliament permitting inclosures in the New Forest dates from 1698. Quite small areas of Open Forest had banks and fences built around them and trees were planted. At South Bentley Inclosure near Fritham you can see the original oak trees planted when these inclosures were made. After a few hundred years South Bentley has begun to take on the character of the ancient woods of the Forest.

Dames Slough Inclosure showing an ancient boundary bank.

In 1851 Parliament passed the Deer Removal Act. This made arrangements for the end of the Forest as a place where deer were farmed for the Crown. The Act of Parliament compensated the Crown for the loss of their deer by allowing much larger areas of Forest to be inclosed for timber production.

The responsibility to grow timber in the Forest was given to the Office of Woods. This branch of government set about clearing the ancient trees from over 1600 hectares of Forest. As well as felling trees and woods large areas of heaths, bogs and fertile lawns were fenced, ploughed and planted using modern industrial forestry techniques.

The impact on the Forest was devastating. Not only was the natural beauty of the Forest being systematically destroyed but the livelihood of the Forest's commoning community was being undermined. The protests of the commoners were joined by a variety of other people who also cared for the Forest, its beauty and people.

The author John Wise wrote a classic book on the Forest, *The New Forest, its history and scenery,* which was published in 1863. Wise wrote about the landscape and way of life of the Forest and appealed both to local residents and the wider British public. The railway meant that the Forest was now accessible to a growing number of people who valued its beauty and open spaces. In 1867 the New Forest Association was formed to promote the conservation of the Forest. The Association is still active today and is recognised as the second oldest amenity society in the world, following the Commons, Open Spaces and Footpath Preservation Society, which was founded in 1865.

At the heart of the protests were some of the Forest's major landowners. These were led by Briscoe Eyre of the Warrens Estate at Bramshaw, Lord Henry Scott (later Lord Montagu of Beaulieu) and William Esdaile of Burley Manor. Their wealth and political power kept the Forest in the public eye and their concerns before Parliament.

The crisis in the Forest came to a head when in 1871 the Office of Woods promoted a Bill to Parliament proposing the complete removal of Forest rights to enable even larger areas to be converted into industrial timber plantations. The Bill failed to get the approval of Parliament. Henry Fawcett MP led the counter attack with a motion to the House of Commons that the felling of all ornamental trees and the making of new inclosures should stop. By 1877 Parliament had passed the New Forest Act which not only recognised the importance of the Forest as a place of amenity and beauty, but also recognised that the rights of Commoners should be respected and managed through the Court of Verderers.

The legacy of the Office of Woods is still very much alive in the modern Forest. The Office of Woods turned into the Forestry Commission who at times have also promoted

Opposite: Inclosures were made for commercial timber growing.

timber plantations at the expense of other interests. The inclosures created under the Deer Removal Act still occupy land that many people think should be Open Forest with commoners' animals grazing through ancient woods, heaths and lawns. For many in the Forest, the Deer Removal Act and the timber inclosures remain an injustice that one day should be put right.

Inclosures reached their greatest extent in the 1960s after forty years of expansion promoted by the Forestry Commission. The economic reasons for making inclosures in the past have now gone. There has also been a realisation that inclosures have caused a great deal of damage to the Forest's wildlife and beauty. Some small areas of inclosures are now being restored to Open Forest, either as heathlands, or as grassy corridors alongside rivers or as grazed open woodlands.

Inclosures are considered to be part of the Open Forest if their fences have been removed, even if some crops of trees are still present. An out-of-date map may well show an inclosure as a conifer plantation but a walk may reveal it to be part of the natural landscape of the Open Forest. As soon as the crops are removed and grazing is restored, the Open Forest landscape rapidly takes back its own.

A few of the inclosures have been managed as woodlands dominated by native trees and cropped in a traditional way. Inclosures such as Churchplace near Ashurst have developed a woodland beauty and value for wildlife that is highly valued and are unlikely to be restored to the Open Forest.

There are well marked footpaths and cycle trails in the inclosures.

Inclosures are very different from enclosures. Enclosures can be found in many places in and around the Forest on what were once privately-owned commons. An enclosure happens where the landowner manages to get the legal power to remove common rights from the land. The landowner may then do with the land whatever he wishes. Around the Forest enclosed land was usually turned into farmland and forestry plantations. There are still places, such as at Setley Common near the Filly Inn south of Brockenhurst, where the land was enclosed but the original heathland landscapes survive.

Enclosures had a dramatic change on the Forest landscape. In the first half of the nineteenth century, private landowners succeeded in enclosing huge areas of commons around the Forest. The Open Forest landscape shrunk dramatically over this period.

Two hundred years ago to the west of today's Open Forest there were heathland commons running around Ringwood across into what is now Dorset. Some of the better soils of the flat lands near the River Avon were also commons, the drier ground being common arable fields and the wetter ground, common hay meadows and pastures. The commoners' animals could cross the Avon at fords such as Watton's Ford and Tyrell's Ford. A tiny fraction of this historic landscape to the west of the Forest survives in places such as Cowards Marsh and Town Common north of Christchurch. Arable fields and hay meadows managed as commons are now completely lost from this part of England.

The Avon in full flood near Christchurch. The heaths of Town Common and St Catherine's Hill run down to the former haymeadows of Winkton Common and the pony-grazed floodplain of Cowards Marsh.

To the east of the Forest the historic open heathland landscapes extended to what are today's Totton and Waterside Towns. Fletchwood Common covered an area from the Crown lands near the Happy Cheese pub to what is now the A326 Totton Western Bypass. Down the Forest Waterside were a series of lanes linking the Open Forest to commons and the saltmarshes of Southampton Water. Places such as Pooks Green and Arters Lawn are fragments of the Open Forest landscape within the farmland enclosures. A survivor of the ancient landscape before enclosure survives at Ashlett by Fawley. Between the Jolly Sailor Pub at Ashlett Creek and the Fawley Power Station Forest ponies still graze the saltmarshes and greens of Southampton Water.

Ashlett Creek in the National Park sits between Fawley Oil Refinery and the Power Station.

19

Who Owns the Open Forest?

There is no definitive map of the Open Forest and there is not a definitive list of who owns it. There are about 50 owners of the Open Forest. The largest landowner by far is the state, which owns over 27,000ha of the National Park of which about 20,000ha are Open Forest.

The Forest land owned by the state is called the Crown land. The Crown land is the historic royal estate which was owned by the monarch as part of the institution of the Crown, rather than his or her personal property. Over time the land has become the responsibility of Government Ministers and their agencies, most recently the Forestry Commission.

Right: The Forestry Commission manage the Crown lands: a wintery scene near Rhinefield.

Below: The Queen's House at Lyndhurst. The office of the Deputy Surveyor.

The civil servant with the particular responsibility for the Crown land is the Deputy Surveyor of the New Forest, who is based in the Queen's House in Lyndhurst. This appears a rather lowly job title for such an important position. The Deputy Surveyor was originally the deputy to the Surveyor General. There has not been a Surveyor General for nearly 200 years, but somehow, the historic job title of deputy in the New Forest has survived.

After the state the next largest landowner of the Open Forest is the National Trust. Over the decades the National Trust has been acquiring privately-owned commons which are next to the Crown land. These are often called the adjacent commons. The National Trust's Open Forest estate includes the Bramshaw Commons, Hightown Common, the Ibsley Commons and Hale Purlieu and runs to over 1200ha. The National Trust estate is still growing and is now looking beyond the Open Forest. A recent purchase at Foxbury plantation near Wellow is a former common, enclosed in 1812 and later planted with a conifer crop. The Trust intends to restore the site to heathland to become a future part of the Forest.

Other parts of the Open Forest are owned by Parish Councils, Hampshire County Council, mineral companies, landed estates, public houses and numerous private individuals. To the walker, or a commoner's animal, the ownership of the land is an invisible layer on what appears to be a large uninterrupted landscape.

Landowners in the Open Forest cannot do with their land whatever they like. This is because some other people have rights to use the Open Forest, regardless of who owns it. The landowner cannot take those rights away nor do anything to stop people exercising those rights. These ancient rights are the rights of common; the people who own and use those rights are known as the commoners.

Cadnam Common from Stagbury Hill: part of the National Trust's estate.

Above: *Foxbury Plantation: an enclosed common to be restored to heathland.*

Left: *The Fighting Cocks at Godshill: one of the private ownerships of the Open Forest.*

THE NEW FOREST COMMONERS

Over the years, New Forest commoners have been the subject of all sorts of speculations, romantic flights of fancy, and academic studies. The practice of commoning is still little understood by many people who come to enjoy the Forest.

What is a New Forest Commoner?

The word 'commoner' in most parts of England is used to mean someone who is not a member of the nobility. We have the House of Commons in Parliament to separate it from the House of Lords. In the New Forest, however, Lords and Ladies can also be commoners.

The word 'commoner' is used in the Forest to describe someone who not only owns common rights, but who also uses those rights. In the Forest, this is referred to as exercising your rights or being a practising commoner. If this means putting grazing animals on the Open Forest, the practice is called 'turning out' or 'depasturing' Forest stock.

The number of practising commoners changes from year to year. There are currently (2000–2005) between 300 and 500 commoners exercising rights at any one time. The commoners are a minority among those who live in the Forest. New Forest commoning does not happen in some remote corner of the country, but among the growing cities and suburbs of one of the most crowded and wealthy parts of England.

The official record of what common rights exist is known as the Atlas of Common Rights. The Atlas began to be drawn up during the disputes of the mid-nineteenth century. The final Atlas was prepared in 1949 and is bound in seven large volumes which are held in the Verderers' Court. The Atlas is a series of maps of enclosed farmland showing individual fields and houses. It is ownership of the properties marked in the Atlas which gives ownership of common rights. The Atlas has great importance as

Opposite: *Commoners at a drift.*

it not only records what land you need to have if you are to use common rights, but also what land you need to have if you are to vote in an election of the Verderers.

The lands with common rights extend way beyond the boundary of the National Park. Properties with common rights can be found in the suburbs of Bournemouth and Southampton as well as among the fields of Cranborne in Dorset and Odstock in Wiltshire.

The Atlas makes a distinction between fields giving common rights on adjacent commons and those fields giving rights over the Crown land of the Open Forest. There are subtle differences between common rights and Forest rights. Everyone exercising those rights calls themselves a commoner. Someone with Forest rights may call themselves a forester. The name forester is sometimes also given to someone who may not exercise common rights but whose work and family connections mean they are part of the community of the working Forest. This is a much older meaning of a word used elsewhere in Britain to refer to someone working in the timber growing industry.

If you have rights to graze just one common it is likely that your animals may wander onto another common or onto the Crown land. As there are no fences between the commons, there is nothing to stop this happening. It is acceptable for animals to wander between commons. This right for animals to roam and graze freely across the whole Open Forest is called the law of vicinage. In practice a commoner of one part of the Open Forest is therefore a commoner of the whole Open Forest.

Opposite: Looking towards Linwood. The changes in land ownership cannot be seen on the ground.

Below: East Boldre and Furzey Lodge. Commoning families still turn out from this area.

Below right: Neighbours to the Open Forest need to have strong hedges.

The Common Rights of the Open Forest

Pasture

The right to graze livestock on the Open Forest. The usual rights are to graze ponies and cattle, but sometimes rights to graze donkeys and sheep are also claimed.

A Highland steer at Longcross.

Pannage, or mast

The right to let pigs out to feed on the Open Forest during the pannage season, which is set annually. The length of the pannage season varies from year to year to allow pigs to eat the acorns which are poisonous to cattle and ponies. The pigs will also eat the abundant crab apples and anything else they can find. On some adjacent commons of the Open Forest there is a right to turn out pigs all year round if they are breeding sows.

The ancient tradition of pigs foraging in the woods.

Above: *Stacked wood in an inclosure.*

Below right: *Turfcutters Arms at East Boldre.*

Below: *Setley marl pits.*

Estovers

The right to collect firewood for fuel. This right was been reduced to protect the timber of the Open Forest. Those commoners with rights of estovers are now provided with stacks of firewood from the timber plantations.

Turbary

The right to cut heathland turfs for fuel. The shallow peaty soils of the wet heaths could be cut and dried to fuel turf fires. This right is no longer exercised; the last few turfs were cut in 1989 at Faircross. Historic records suggest that very large areas of the wet heaths of the Open Forest were once cut for fuel. The practice of turf cutting is remembered in the pub sign at East Boldre.

Marl

The right to dig clay from the Open Forest to spread on fields. This right is also no longer exercised. Marl pits are clay pits where the clay is rich in fossil shells. Marl was once an important soil improver on fields around the Forest.

Why is New Forest Commoning Special?

Until the Industrial Revolution, commoning was a way of life for many communities in much of lowland England. Forest commoning is one of the strongholds of this type of land management and dates back before written records were kept. The importance of commoning in the New Forest is that the tradition has survived on a large scale, and in doing so, helps to manage a treasured landscape and place rich in wildlife.

Most counties in the country have commons. In upland counties, the practice of commoning is still widespread. In north and west Scotland, commoning, in the form of crofting, is still a major part of the rural economy. In many counties in southern England the commons have survived, but the commoning way of life has all but died out. There are still working commons and commoners scattered around lowland England but nowhere else on the scale of the New Forest. This survival has happened without Forest commoning becoming like something from a living museum. Commoning today is different from how it was 200 years ago, and very different from 500 years ago, but Forest commoning is still an important part of our cultural heritage.

The cattle and ponies owned by the commoners have been called 'the architects of the Forest'. The most important habitats of the Forest and most of the special landscapes need grazing to keep them in good condition. Without grazing, the open landscapes of heaths and bogs of the Open Forest would fill up with rough grass and trees. The sunny glades of the Forest's ancient woodlands would close over and the woodlands become very dark. Without grazing animals, the Open Forest landscapes would become much more wooded, poorer in wildlife and very difficult to walk through.

A Forest architect at work.

Ecologists now think that natural landscapes in lowland Europe are those where large grazing animals are free to roam. Thousands of years ago before farmers starting looking after animals, the land which is now the New Forest would have been home to wild ponies and cattle. These wild animals became extinct about 3500 years ago and were replaced by farmed animals.

Just outside the National Park, at Testwood Lakes in Totton, archaeologists have recently found remains of giant wild cattle called Aurochen, which were living alongside Bronze Age people and their farm animals. Cows have therefore been a part of the Forest landscape for a very long time. Forest commoning is ecologically important because it provides the grazing animals which continue to shape the landscape and habitats of the Open Forest.

The Commoners' Animals

Every animal on the Open Forest is owned by someone. Unlike in conventional farming, Forest commoners' animals are free to roam over a landscape, where animals owned by different people mix together. The commoners' animals are the ponies, cattle, sheep, donkeys and pigs. Other animals such as rabbits and the introduced species of deer, together with wild animals such as roe deer, all belong to the landowners.

Born on the Forest.

The commoners' animals are not wild. These are farm animals which live out in the wide open spaces of the Open Forest. There are some ponies which are born on the heath and are rarely handled. There are other animals which may be born on a farm and then turned out into the Open Forest for a year or two before being brought back to the farm to be prepared to be sold. If winter feed runs short on a commoner's holding, there is always the option of turning out the cattle to feed on heathers and the early spring growth of the Forest's wetlands. Each commoner will find their own way to make best use of the land available to their animals.

The Open Forest is a feminine place. Bulls, boars and rams have no right to be on the Open Forest. Stallions are permitted, but only between May and July, and their numbers are carefully regulated. The only male domestic animals which can be seen year round are Jack donkeys. Recent experiments in the Netherlands have created landscapes with a natural balance of male and female animals grazing together all year round. Herds of bachelor bulls and stallions create areas of bare ground and broken vegetation on a scale which is absent from the Forest. The Open Forest is a wild landscape which reflects the unnatural absence of bulls and stallions.

Commoners' animals can roam wherever they like, but in practice most don't. Ponies form extended family groups, often led by an older mare. The group uses an area of the Forest which provides them with their daily needs. The ponies need somewhere to feed using different food at different times of year. The young ponies learn from the family group how to eat winter food such as gorse and holly. Ponies need shelter from winter winds and from the biting flies of a still summer day.

A group of ponies relaxing in the sunshine.

31

The family group carries the knowledge of the best places. A good reliable supply of water is essential year round and this can come from bogs, ponds and streams. Groups of ponies have latrine areas where they dung but don't graze. This behaviour helps protect them from parasites building up in the grasses which they eat. The area of Forest used by a pony is called its 'haunt'. A commoner will know the haunts of their animals and so can keep an eye on them through the year.

In 2005, the most abundant of the commoners' animals were the ponies, with 4,302 turned out. Most ponies are related to the New Forest breed but locally Shetland ponies are popular. There were also 2609 cattle which were nearly all beef cattle. The Open Forest was also home to 97 donkeys, 194 pigs and about 40 sheep. A visitor wanting to see ponies and cattle need only take a short walk anywhere in the Open Forest. Pigs, donkeys and sheep tend to be found year round on the adjacent commons, such as around Bramshaw.

The Administration of Commoning

The exercising of common rights on the Open Forest has its own bureaucracy and red tape. With hundreds of people together with thousands of animals sharing the same piece of ground, it is necessary for there to be rules and for people to work together.

Marking Fees

Having common rights gives a commoner the legal right to graze the Open Forest, but this right does not come for free. Anyone who turns out an animal on the Forest must pay an annual marking fee. Marking fees are payable for every animal, the more animals turned out, the more fees paid. Marking fees help pay for the administration of commoning. A pony will cost between £9 and £20, and a cow between £2.50 and £20.

Drifts

Drifting.

Marking fees help pay the wages of Forest officers called Agisters. Agisters organise 'drifts', or round-ups, which are important occasions in the life of the Forest. There are about 40 drifts a year, running from the end of summer into autumn. Over the course of the year there will be a drift in every part of the Forest. At a drift a group of commoners will ride across the Open Forest rounding-up the free living ponies. The ponies are driven along a Forest boundary such as a fence to a place where they can be held safely. Forest drifts are very much a part of what makes the Forest special, but they are not unique. A Forest drift may be seen as the equivalent to shepherds rounding up their sheep with sheepdogs on a common on the Lakeland fells.

Left: *The drift at Turf Hill.*

Below left: *A hair cut tells that marking fees have been paid.*

Below: *Different tail cuts denote which region of the Forest a pony belongs to.*

Once the ponies have been rounded up and held in the pound, the Agister checks the records that the marking fee has been paid for each animal. On payment the long hairs of the pony's tail are cut in a fashion unique to that Agister's part of the Forest.

Having a pony held in a pound gives an opportunity to check the health of the animal. A pony in the pound can be treated with medicine to control intestinal worms or other parasites. If an Agister is unhappy about the health of an animal, they may insist that the animal is taken off the Forest until it is well enough to return.

In the pound.

Not all animals return to the Open Forest after a drift. This is a perfect time for commoners to bring their animals home or take them to market. In recent years there has been a trend away from selling ponies straight from the Open Forest. Some commoners prefer to keep the ponies in fields until they are used to being handled or even ready to be ridden. This way the market value of the ponies is greatly improved.

Drifts are important events in the social life of the commoning community. They are hard work, requiring skill and knowledge in handling animals which are not tame. Riding across the Open Forest, rounding up and driving herds of free-living ponies requires great skills of horsemanship. This is horse riding not as a sport but as part of a living tradition and a practical solution to an annual task. Those who are not riding can help at the pound, guiding the animals into the holding pens and assisting the Agisters in their work.

Drifts are not public events, but once a year riding skills are tested in public at the annual Point to Point. This is held every Boxing Day at a different place in the Forest. Spectators gather around the finishing post which is advertised beforehand in the local newspapers. Competitors know the point where the race will finish but the starting point is a well-kept secret.

Racing to the finish line at the Boxing Day Point to Point.

At the last minute on the morning of the event, the competitors are told where to meet up. This gives the first clue as to where the starting point is. Then the race is on, and the surest horse and rider with the best knowledge of the Forest will win. There is no set route, local knowledge and quick thinking is required to navigate the bogs, road underpasses, inclosure fences and all the other hurdles along the way. All those who complete the course receive equal admiration. Attending the Point to Point is a fitting way to conclude the Forest year.

Brands and Sales

At drifts a special effort is made to round up the foals that have been born on the Forest. This is called colt hunting. The foals and their mothers may be taken off the Forest to be sold. If the foal is to live out on the Open Forest it is branded.

Branding is essential to help identify who owns which animal. Branding is done with a hot metal branding iron pressed against the skin of the pony, leaving a permanent scar. This is a quick process which does not seem to cause the animals any lasting distress. Each commoner has their own unique brand made up of letters, numbers and symbols. The simple, bold designs of the brands mean that the marks are easily recognised and can be read at a distance. The Agisters know all the brands so they know who owns every animal in their part of the Forest.

Pony sales occur five times a year, with one sale in the spring and then other sales at the time of the drifts. The sales are social gatherings for the commoners as well as for everyone with an interest in horses and the life of the Forest. Everyone is welcome. The sales are held near Beaulieu Road Station, among the bogs and heaths of Denny, and opposite the bar of the Beaulieu Road Hotel. The sales area has been recently rebuilt to meet modern standards. The traditional wooden yards and pounds have been upgraded but still hold onto their functional, homemade character. Even when there is no sale, the yards at Beaulieu Road Station are well worth visiting as an example of functional, vernacular architecture.

Above: *A collection of brands.*

Right: *At the Beaulieu Road sales.*

THE VERDERERS AND AGISTERS

Oyez, Oyez, Oyez

All manner of persons who have any presentment to make, or matter or thing to do at this Court of Verderers, let them come forward and they shall be heard. God save the Queen.

The call to order made by an Agister as crier of the Court from the dock each time the Court sits in public session.

Establishment and History

The Verderers' Court as we know it today came into existence after decades of bitter disputes between the civil servants in the Office of Woods and the people of the Forest. These struggles for power over the Crown lands resulted in Parliament passing the New Forest Act 1877, which not only created the modern Court of Verderers but is also the legal foundation for the conservation of the Open Forest's landscape and wildlife.

Who are the Verderers and How do You Get to be One?

It is the role of the Verderers to regulate how the Open Forest is managed. In doing this the Verderers both control and protect commoning and help preserve the beauty and special character of the Open Forest.

The position of Verderer is one of great responsibility and prestige. At any one time there are only 10 Verderers, half of whom are appointed and the other half elected.

The senior Verderer, who chairs the Court, is called the Official Verderer. The Official Verderer represents the Queen and is a Crown appointment. In recent years this post

An Agister in uniform.

Photo supplied by kind permission
of the New Forest Verderers

has been held by a Forest landowner who has experience in business or the law. Of the other appointed Verderers one is chosen by the Forestry Commission. The two most recent Forestry Commission Verderers have been the eldest sons of Forest landowners.

The beauty and enjoyment of the Forest is the particular role of the Amenity Verderer, who is appointed by Natural England, a government agency. There is a Verderer appointed by the National Park Authority which is the local planning authority, and also a Verderer appointed by the Department of the Environment, Food and Rural Affairs (DEFRA).

The Verderers sitting in court. The Verderers are on the bench. The Forestry Commission officers are invited to sit at the table below the bench.

Photo supplied by kind permission
of the New Forest Verderers

In addition to the five appointed Verderers there are five elected Verderers. The elected Verderers are usually people who exercise their common rights and are well known in the commoning community. An elected Verderer serves for six years.

To vote at a Verderers' election, or to stand for election, you need to hold property which has common rights attached. There are many thousands of houses with common rights, including substantial parts of the suburbs of the towns outside the Forest. Not everyone with common rights may stand or vote. There is a property qualification that you also need to own or rent at least one acre (0.40ha) of land with common rights. If you have that property you can ask to be added to the Forest's electoral register. With the property qualification, the Verderers elections are one of the last remnants of an historic electoral system based not on 'one man, one vote' but on the ownership of property.

Left: *Much of Ringwood is built on land with common rights.*

Below: *The Verderers' Hall and the Queen's House.*

What Happens at the Court?

The full title of the Court of Verderers is the Courts of Attachment and Swainmote. When meeting as the Court of Swainmote, the Verderers sit as a magistrates' court and judge alleged offences against the Forest. The Court can hold a trial and convict people of offences. The Court of Swainmote has not sat for many years. The Court prefers to pursue prosecutions through the conventional Magistrates' Court in Lyndhurst or Southampton.

The regular Verderers' Court, the Court of Attachment, is much less formal than a trial. It has a similar feel to a busy Parish Council meeting. The meetings are open to all and many people turn up to see the Forest's business being done. The Court meets in the Verderers' Hall, part of the Queen's House at Lyndhurst. A little like the Verderers themselves, the hall is a Victorian construction based on ancient foundations, updated with a few modern conveniences.

The Verderers sit at the end of the hall along a high bench backed by a copy of the Royal Coat of Arms of 1669. Below the Verderers' bench are lower benches set around a table where Forestry Commission officers sit. To the left of the Court is the dock. This short set of steps and small platform is made of rough hewn oak and is reputed to be 500 years old. When the Court sat as Swainmote, the accused would stand in the dock and be presented to the Court, so statements from the dock have become known as presentments.

Above and below: The Crown Stirrup pub.

A Reminder of Forest Laws

This large stirrup hangs in the Verderers' Hall, a reminder of past Forest laws. A dog which was too large to pass through the stirrup would have some of its toes amputated before it was allowed onto the Open Forest. This mutilation was called 'expedition' and prevented the local dogs from disturbing the Crown's deer and other Forest creatures. The Crown and Stirrup appear in a local pub name on the Brockenhurst road out of Lyndhurst.

Right: The stirrup.

The dock is now used by all who wish to make a presentment to the Court. Walking into the dock and speaking to the Verderers sitting high on their bench is a memorable experience. The use of the dock for presentments is something new. Within living memory, presentments were made by walking to the fireplace in the Hall and speaking from there.

Before presentments are received, the Court is called to order by the senior Agister in his uniform of dark green jacket, gold buttons, buff riding breeches and high black boots. The court deals with administrative matters and makes announcements of decisions arising from previous presentments. Presentments may be made by anyone as long as the business relates to the many responsibilities of the Court in the Forest. Some of the more substantial presentments are from local authorities or the Forestry Commission seeking to undertake works on the Forest. The proposals are all made in public and there is a chance for all to comment. The Court is an invaluable place to witness how the Forest community feels about the issues of the day.

Day-to-day, the Verderers regulate how the commons of the Open Forest are managed. At the Court reports on the Open Forest are presented by the Agisters. The Verderers employ the Agisters, five men who look over the commons checking that all the grazing animals have had their marking fees paid and are in a fit condition to be out. This work is often carried out on horseback as that is the easiest way to get around. An Agister has the authority to insist that a sick animal is taken off the Forest.

Animals are at risk from thoughtless driving.

The Agisters also have the distressing job of attending traffic accidents and helping the emergency services dealing with injured animals. A report on animal accidents is given at each Verderers' Court. The main roads across the Forest have been fenced but animals are free to wander along the minor roads. Speed limits have been introduced that have helped to reduce accidents. Every driver in the Forest needs to take special care and give animals the space they need. Agisters are usually practising commoners who know their neighbours and their animals. There can be few other jobs in the British court system which require the officer to have such a detailed knowledge of a wild open landscape and of the people and the animals which live there.

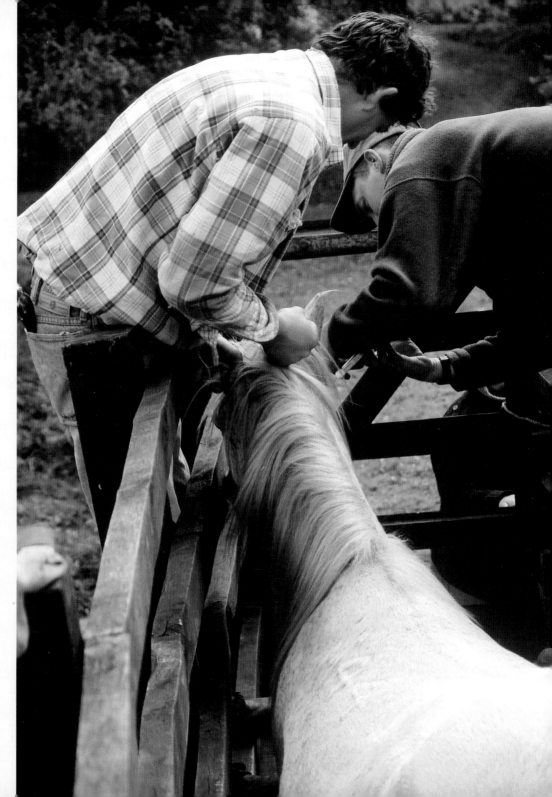

Agisters at work at a drift. They are giving a pony medicine to control parasites.

It is in the Verderers' Court that the dates of the pannage season are announced by the Forestry Commission on behalf of the Crown. The pannage season is the period of time when all commoners with the right of mast may let their pigs run free throughout the Open Forest. This season changes from year to year depending on how heavy the mast, or crop of acorns, has been. Each year a judgement has to be made as to what risk there is to cattle and ponies from acorn poisoning. The pigs eat the acorns and so a heavy mast year usually means a longer pannage season.

Pannage in the woods: Fritham.

As well as regulating how the commoners use the Forest, the Verderers also have a major influence on what the landowners of the Open Forest may do. As the representatives of the Crown, the Forestry Commission generate a regular flow of proposed works on the Open Forest. These may be substantial, such as the creation of a new caravan site, or something as small as agreeing a route for an underground telephone line to a cottage in the Forest. The Verderers' consent is needed for almost anything which may impact on the ability to exercise a right of common or on the beauty of the Forest.

The work of the court is varied and it takes a great deal of dedication to be a Verderer. The role is unpaid and a huge amount of work happens outside the public meetings. The Verderers are supported by a paid clerk but the Court runs itself on a very small budget. The Court changes to meet the changing world, for example a recent new role of the Verderers has been the administration of a Countryside Stewardship scheme which provides financial support to help commoners maintain the Forest herds of ponies and cattle.

The Verderers' Court is a direct descendant from the ancient Forest courts which governed the medieval landscape. Parliament has given the Verderers an unrivalled responsibility for the Open Forest and inclosures within what is now the New Forest National Park.

Forestry Commission campsites on the Open Forest need the Verderers' permission.

MANAGING THE OPEN FOREST

The landowners of the Open Forest have the responsibility of managing the landscape. The responsibilities of the Forestry Commission as the manager of the state-owned land are set out under the various New Forest Acts of Parliament. The private landowners have different responsibilities mostly arising from other Acts of Parliament. As the Open Forest is a Site of Special Scientific Interest (SSSI), landowners are now obliged to maintain the Open Forest in a 'favourable condition'. In practice the majority of Open Forest management is undertaken by the Forestry Commission.

Deer

For much of the history of the Forest deer have been the most prestigious of animals. The right to hunt deer was a closely guarded privilege, only to be enjoyed by royalty and those they favoured. The deer herds were an important living larder. It was only about 150 years ago, with the controversial Deer Removal Act, that the carefully managed herds of deer became relegated to their current role.

There are five species of deer on the Open Forest. Roe deer are a native wild animal and have been a part of the Forest landscape since the last Ice Age. Red deer are also native but the current herds in the Forest were introduced after the native herds became extinct. Fallow deer are not native but have a long pedigree as an animal living wild in the Forest. The exact date of their introduction to the Forest is unknown, but it is thought to be in the Norman-medieval period, some 900 years ago. Sika deer and muntjac are relative newcomers having been introduced by shooting estates and as curiosities over the last hundred years.

Deer have no natural predators in the Open Forest. Traffic accidents kill some deer every year, but without management their populations would be controlled by the natural processes of disease and starvation.

Opposite: *A red deer stag bellowing during the rut.*

Below: *A roe buck.*

A sika stag in Frame Wood.

The Death of William Rufus

On 2 August, 1100, an arrow killed King William II while he was hunting deer somewhere in the New Forest, and his death has been the subject of speculation and conspiracy theories for over 900 years. Even the site of his death has been questioned. Did he die in the Forest glade at Canterton now marked by the Rufus Stone, or was it somewhere in the countryside near Beaulieu? Did the arrow which killed him come from an assassin, or was it an accident?

William Rufus certainly had his enemies. When his father William the Conqueror died he gave Robert, his eldest son, the Duchy of Normandy and he gave William his land in England. The youngest of the three brothers, Henry, inherited 5000 pounds of silver. After years of quarrelling and rebellions, Robert pawned Normandy to William in exchange for money to pay for Robert joining the First Crusade to Jerusalem. On William's death, Robert regained Normandy.

Among the hunting party when Rufus was killed was Sir Walter Tyrell, who fled the scene immediately after the incident. Folk history tells that he rode westwards crossing the River Avon and eventually found refuge in France. One of the legends tells that he persuaded a local blacksmith to take the shoes off his horse and replace them back to front to confuse anyone following him. Henry, on hearing of the death of his brother, went straight to Winchester where the Royal treasury was stored and within three days he was crowned King.

The body of William Rufus was left where he died. Folk history tells that it was discovered by a local man called Purkis, who put the body in his cart and carried it to Romsey and then to Winchester. Nine hundred years later William's bones are still in Winchester Cathedral. Above the choir stalls are a series of ancient boxes holding assorted last remains of royalty. William's bones are mixed with those of the Saxon King Canute and Canute's wife Emma.

HERE STOOD THE OAK TREE, ON WHICH AN ARROW SHOT BY SIR WALTER TYRRELL AT A STAG, GLANCED AND STRUCK KING WILLIAM THE SECOND, SURNAMED RUFUS, ON THE BREAST, OF WHICH HE INSTANTLY DIED, ON THE SECOND DAY OF AUGUST, ANNO 1100.

The Rufus Stone stands opposite the Sir Walter Tyrell pub at Canterton near Brook. The eighteenth-century stone memorial is inside the nineteenth-century cast iron case.

Deer management on the Open Forest is one on the ways which landowners can influence grazing pressures. A careful balance has to be struck between the welfare of the deer and the responsibilities of the landowners to their land and their neighbours. Deer are much-loved creatures and many visitors in the Forest enjoy seeing them at the Boldrewood sanctuary. Deer meat (venison) is an enjoyable part of the Forest menu; it is a lean meat ideal for roasts, stews and pies.

Below: *The various colour forms of fallow deer can be seen at Boldrewood sanctuary.*

Below right: *Fallow fawns at Boldrewood.*

A local celebration of deer: Cadnam.

It is the job of the 12 Forestry Commission keepers to manage the deer populations. In the modern Forest, the rifle has replaced the wolf as the method of control. Each keeper has his beat, an area of Forest which he must get to know in great detail. In spring the number of deer are counted and a judgement is made on what natural food is available to support them. The numbers vary from year to year, but on the Crown land the current plan is to keep the population at 1200 fallow, 400 roe, 100 sika, 100 red and to try to shoot all muntjac. Shooting, or culling, deer happens all year round except during the mating season – the rut – in October.

With patience and a little luck, a quiet walk anywhere in the Forest will bring a reasonable chance of seeing deer. Around the full moon in October a night time walk can be rewarded by the eerie roars of the stags. It is best to keep well clear of the stags during the rut. Usually deer are approachable and some herds are very calm when they see people; others are hesitant and can rapidly disappear into the heath and woods.

Fire

Heathlands are habitats which can burn. Fire is a natural occurrence on heathlands, and heathland wildlife is able to cope with occasional burns. Fire is a useful tool to keep the heathlands in an attractive condition for people, wildlife and grazing animals. A good fire will create a flush of young growth on grasses, heathers and gorse and will rejuvenate the heathland.

Above: *Fire is carefully managed to encourage the fresh growth of grass and heather.*

Left: *Ian Young and other keepers set a controlled burn of heather and gorse.*

Wildlife Following Fire

Fire brings with it dramatic changes in the habitats of the heath. The dominant grasses and heathers are reduced to the same height as the smaller plants. There is at first a lot of bare ground and ash. The heath starts to regrow in the spring following the fire.

The young heather in the first year is particularly vulnerable to dodder, a parasitic plant. Dodder seeds germinate on the bare ground among the ashes, and the seedling reaches up towards other plants. If a heather bush is touched then the seedling injects itself into the soft tissues of the stem. As soon as the dodder has a grip its roots die away and the whole plant lives by feeding on the sap of the heather. The brilliant red strands of the dodder form a shining waxy web over the heath.

The parasite dodder in full flower.

Marsh gentians grow on heaths which are wet in winter and which never really dry out in high summer. The gentians are small trailing plants which are easily overgrown by the tougher plants on the heath. Fire brings an opportunity to bloom. The plants thrive in the bare ground, growing in size and strength. It may be two or three years after a fire before the plants are big enough to flower. If the ponies and cattle keep grazing back the grasses then the gentian may continue to bloom for many years. Gentian flowers are some of the brightest, richest blues in nature.

The silver studded blue butterfly is a heathland specialist. Its caterpillars are fussy eaters, liking a particular type of heather. Old heather is too woody for them; they prefer the soft green growth which occurs in the first few years after a burn. Grazing then helps keep the heather short and young and holds back the even more vigorous purple moor grass. Silver studded blues can be found on nearly every heath on the Forest. They seem able to survive as low populations in the older heathers, but this can rapidly expand to hundreds of butterflies flying together when the conditions are right.

Above: *Marsh gentian blooming amongst the purple moor grass.*

Left: *Silver studded blue butterfly.*

Heathland fires can be terribly destructive and dangerous. A bad fire can burn away dry heathland soils, turning good grazing into parched thin grassland, and can encourage the spread of bracken. Fires which are too hot can burn away the soil and remove the seeds and eggs of future generations of wildlife. Creatures which cannot move quickly enough to escape the fire will be consumed by the flames. A bad fire will also threaten the lives and homes of people in the Forest. The worst fires are uncontrolled fires in summer.

Fires on the Forest need to be carefully managed. Each year there is a discussion as to what areas of heath would benefit from burning. A heath may be burnt about every twenty-five years. The ideas of where to burn next usually start with commoners talking to Forestry Commission keepers. The ideas then get discussed with the Verderers and Natural England who consider the value of the fire for landscape and wildlife as well as to improve grazing. Finally the ideas get discussed by the Open Forest Advisory Committee which advises the Deputy Surveyor.

Burning is undertaken by a specialist team of Forestry Commission workers. A burn, like a drift, is part of the cultural life of the Forest. Before a burn happens, the boundary is marked out by cutting the heather around the outside; this is called a trace. The trace helps to keep the fire where it is meant to be. Fires are usually started to burn into the wind and the fire moves slowly forward. A line of workers and vehicles with emergency water tanks wait ready to stop the fire from straying. Burns happen in the drier winter months. A good dry week with a steady wind after winter rain is perfect burning weather when there is dry heather but wet soil.

After a fire the heath can look bleak and uninviting. However the fires reveal archaeological remains so faint that the slightest cover of heather hides them. Bronze Age round barrow burial mounds may stand out clearly in the heaths, but the much lower disc barrows and boundaries of ancient farmed landscapes can only be seen after a burn. A shower of rain washes away the ashes and can reveal scatters of flints worked by people living in the Forest during the Stone Age. Some of the larger gorse stands are associated with areas disturbed by people. Gorse is abundant in places like old gravel pits but also on medieval fields once farmed but now part of the heath. Burns on places like Beaulieu Heath reveal a pattern of abandoned hedge banks for the short time until the rejuvenated gorse grows back.

Cutting

As well as being burnt, the vegetation of the Open Forest is also cut.

Cutting Bracken

Bracken is the most common and most vigorous fern growing on the Open Forest. The cutting of bracken has been carefully controlled throughout history to protect it. When cut in late summer, bracken provides winter bedding for animals kept in barns over winter. The following spring the mixture of dung and bracken-rich bedding makes excellent manure. Cutting bracken for bedding still occurs on a small scale, as does cutting to provide a substitute for straw in the garden for growing strawberries and other crops. On a much larger scale, bracken is harvested by machines and composted. Bracken breaks down into a fine organic compost useful in the specialist nursery trade for growing acid-loving plants and more generally as a peat substitute.

Cut bracken is not only useful in its own right but cutting also controls the vigour of the fern, allowing a mass of fine grasses and flowers to grow beneath its shade. Bracken areas provide good late summer feed for Forest animals as well as a spectacular flush of spring flowers including one of the Forest's specialities, wild gladioli. Uncut bracken stands can become very uninteresting places with a deep thatch of dead fronds that blanket out the grasses, flowers and everything else beneath their canopy.

Below left: *Near South Bentley the old airfield provides a base for composting bracken.*

Below: *Wild gladiolus in its bracken habitat.*

Heather bales at South Bentley.

Cutting Heather

Old heather is not always burnt. Heather can also be cut and baled like straw. A bale of heather is a tough woody bundle which is light to lift when dry but strong and resistant to rot when wet. The practice of thatching Forest cottages with heather has died out but the tradition of using heather continues. In recent years a new use has been found for heather in repairing damaged wetlands. A drain in unstable soils can start to erode away neighbouring bogs and grasslands. Anchoring heather bales into the drain slows down the flow of the water and traps the sand and gravel. This simple technique has proved invaluable in recent years in repairing damaged wetlands in a gentle and natural way.

Above: *A river restored.*

Above right: *The old engineered channel remains as a still backwater.*

Cutting Holly

On a hot summer's day, holly woods cast an intense dark shade and are a favourite place for ponies to shelter from the sun. The holly woods, or holms, have a dense canopy of thick waxy leaves rising above the bleached, silvery, contorted trunks. The gnarled and twisted character of the holly trees is partially due to them sometimes being burnt as part of the heath and partially due to the practices of pollarding and coppicing. In winter ponies chew the soft bark of the trees, adding to their rugged character.

Pollarding and coppicing are the same sort of thing but happen at different heights. A pollard is a tree which has had its branches cut off above the reach of the mouths of Forest animals. This way the cut branches will regrow quickly as they are not grazed. The tree trunk with the top cut off is called a bole, or boling.

Above: *Bramshaw Great Wood: holly and ancient beeches.*

Left: *Holly pollards on the open heath at Broomy Plain.*

A coppiced tree is cut at ground level and so grows back much more slowly as Forest animals eat the young growth. This grazing rarely kills the tree but it slows down the regrowth. The low cut stump is called a stool. Most holly areas have a mixture of pollards and stools. At the sound of chainsaws on a cold winter day, Forest animals will gather to feed on the green leaves and soft bark of the freshly-cut holly.

Holly cutting happens in the depth of winter. The cutting was historically done to provide green leaves for deer to graze on when everything else had died away. The leaves high in the hollies can be round and soft, very different from the prickly defences on the lower branches. In recent years the tradition has been revived on a large scale. Commoners like cutting holly because it provides winter food for animals in the shelter of the woodlands.

Naturalists like cutting holly because it temporarily lifts the shade of the wood allowing specialist wildlife, particularly lichens, to thrive on the trunks of ancient trees. People who like landscape like holly being cut because it maintains another of the special working landscapes of the Forest. After a period of conflicts between commoners and conservationists in the 1980s, cutting holly was found to be something that everyone could agree on.

Nearly all native trees in the Forest respond well to pollarding. Many of the finest ancient beech and oak trees were once cut in this way. The historic practice of pollarding lives on. Scattered around the Forest are stands of young pollards which for one reason or another have been cut by those honouring the tradition.

Cutting ancient pollards is something that can be done to prolong the life of ancient trees. In other Forests in South England, such as Hatfield Forest and Epping Forest, this is done as there are few ancient trees and every effort is made to keep those they have alive until the next generation can take their place. In the New Forest, it is estimated that there are likely to be over a quarter of a million ancient trees with many more growing to maturity. It is good to keep the tradition of pollarding alive in the New Forest, but there is no particular economic or wildlife conservation reason to do so.

The ancient trees of the Forest are among the largest living things that most of us will ever meet. The history of cutting often creates a scarred and pitted trunk. Contorted limbs, far bigger than the trunks of most other trees, branch outwards and upwards towards the light. Some trees rot to become hollow, living drums; others grow into their neighbours so that two may be spliced as one. Each tree has a unique character reflecting a lifetime longer than we can easily imagine. No trip to the Forest is complete without a walk through the groves of ancient trees.

Beech pollards in the Ancient and Ornamental woods at Bratley.

Cutting out Aliens

The Forest has many beautiful gardens stocked with plants from all over the world. The timber inclosures have also provided opportunities to grow trees from climates similar to Britain. This introduction of plants not native to the Forest has resulted in a few species doing incredibly well.

A species that breaks out of its garden or plantation to colonise the wild landscapes of the Forest is called an alien. Many alien plants gain a foothold in the Forest and become an interesting and accepted part of the landscape. A few species are so successful that they can overwhelm the things that make the Forest special and therefore need to be controlled. Two close relatives of our native heathers have become a problem, these are a rhododendron from the Pontus mountains in Turkey and a gaultheria from western North America.

Above: *Uncontrolled rhododendron can shade out Forest wildlife.*

Right: *Clearing gaultheria requires considerable effort and investment.*

THE WILDLIFE OF THE OPEN FOREST

The Open Forest is an exceptional place for nature; there really is nowhere quite like it. The importance is now recognised under European law and international treaties. The vocabulary of the Forest now includes the titles of these designations. These are Ramsar treaty sites, Special Protection Areas, Special Areas of Conservation and Sites of Special Scientific Interest.

There are five groups of habitats for which the Open Forest is recognised as having international importance. These habitats are its bogs, its heaths, its ponds, its woods, and its rivers. These habitats are not found separated from one another but merge together across the landscape as part of an ever-changing tapestry.

Bogs

Soldier's Bog north of Burley.

Anyone walking for any length of time on the Open Forest will encounter one of its many bogs. Usually bogs are in the low-lying valley bottoms, but they can also be found on hill sides where natural spring lines keep the soil constantly wet. No two Forest bogs are exactly the same and one part of a bog can be different from the next. There are bogs within ancient woodlands and bogs in the middle of wide sunny heaths.

In some places the bogs are very acid and in others the water comes from springs rich in minerals. The more acid bogs can have spectacular multi-coloured mats of bog mosses. Where the water is slightly more nutrient rich black bog rush and reeds are found as well as great rarities such as bog sedge and slender cotton-grass. Most bogs are very wet but still firm underfoot. There are others where spring heads on the edge of a bog, locally called clay boils, can trap the boot of a careless walker. Occasionally bogs have formed over ponds with just a thin layer of floating mosses; these bogs quake and swing when stepped on and are best avoided.

The Forest has more bogs, of greater variety, than any other part of lowland western Europe. There are about 90 separate bog systems in 20 river catchments covering about 3000ha.

Heaths

Bogs need high quality water which is not polluted by fertilisers from farmland or sewage works. Forest bogs are of a particularly high quality as most of the water flowing into them comes from the surrounding heathlands. The Forest heaths are the largest area of heathland in lowland Britain. The complex of heaths and bogs extends to over 17,000ha. In some places the boundary between the heath and the bog can be dramatic, such as miniature cliffs cut by the springs along the side of Soldier's Bog north of Burley. In other places the change is gradual, such as in the bogs under Matley Wood.

Ponies and cattle grazing across the landscape follow narrow paths along the boundary between heath and bog. Their hooves scuff the soil creating bare peaty patches which are ideal conditions for plants such as the marsh clubmoss and the brown beaked sedge. The heathers and moor grasses of the wetter heaths provide plenty of roughage in the ponies' diet, which in turn creates an intriguing ecosystem driven by the rotting down of vegetarian dung.

Sundews are abundant in the bogs and wet heaths. The plant traps and digests insects on its glistening sticky hairs.

Birds of the Heath

As the largest area of lowland heath in the country, it is not surprising that the Forest has some of Britain's best populations of heathland birds.

Both the adult and chick woodlark are camouflaged to live in bare open heathland.

The year starts early for the woodlark. This bird of the open heaths starts singing and establishing a nest site as the days grow longer in February. Woodlarks nest on the ground, preferring very short vegetation or even bare sandy places. Both the adults and the chicks are beautifully camouflaged.

Opposite: Nightfall in late May is a good time to listen for nightjars.

Another master of camouflage is the nightjar. Unlike the woodlark, the nightjar starts breeding much later and has young right through to the summer months. Nightjars nest on the ground, often in a little cover such as along the heathland edge of a birch wood or amongst a bracken stand in the open heath. Nightjars get their name from the churring-whirring call which the adults make in the hour around dusk. The displays of the nightjar are spectacular with birds calling, flashing white wing patches and clapping their wings over their backs.

Dartford warblers are colourful, if a little scruffy, birds of the open heath. The Dartford warbler does not lay its eggs on the ground but makes a nest low down in gorse bushes. The Forest supports at least a third of the British breeding population with over 500 pairs. As well as breeding on the heaths, the occasional pair have set up home in the gorse of coastal grazing marshes. The Dartford warbler is often seen in gorse breaks along with the equally colourful, but more dapper, stonechat.

The populations of nightjars, woodlark and Dartford warblers are all internationally important. In addition the Forest is of great importance for other ground-nesting birds such as lapwing, curlew, redshank, snipe and meadow pipit. These birds are vulnerable to disturbance when they are setting up their nests and rearing their young. People enjoying the Forest can easily put nests at risk, particularly if they let their dogs run free across the heaths.

Burning and grazing create ideal habitats for Dartford warblers.

The stonechat is one of the easiest heathland birds to see as it sits on top of gorse bushes. Its alarm call sounds like two pebbles being knocked together.

High above the heath, hobbies rear their young in abandoned crows' nests. This small falcon spends its winters in Africa south of the Sahara, arriving in the Forest in late spring and early summer. The hobby is a spectacularly agile bird feeding over the bogs catching and eating dragonflies in flight. The acrobatic skills of the hobby are shown off during their courtship displays in April and May, when birds spin, loop-the-loop and pass food to one another.

As the hobbies leave in October, elsewhere in the Forest a much larger bird of prey gathers. This is the hen harrier, which in winter roosts on the Forest heaths. Arriving at dusk and leaving at dawn, these birds feed in the countryside which surrounds the Forest. Their food includes a wide range of small birds as well as reptiles and small mammals.

Having fed mostly on insects following their migration from Africa, hobbies mostly raise their young on a diet of swallows and martins.

Situated in a relatively mild but not too wet part of Europe, the Forest's heaths have more in common with similar habitats in France than in East Anglia or South West England. The heaths are varied and can range from dry grassy areas with a little heather to peaty bog edges. There are four species of heather native to the Forest, the rarest being the Dorset heath, which is confined to the heaths near Burley: the other species are common heather or ling, cross-leaved heath and bell heather. The Forest tends to be a claggy place. Heathland soils are mostly cold wet gravels and clay with only occasional dry sandy banks.

Snakes on the Heath

The Forest's heaths are home to all three species of snake native to Britain; the adder, the grass snake, and the smooth snake.

Early in the day adders bask on hedge banks and in open areas in the heaths.

The grass snake is often seen in and around heathland pools and bogs. Grass snakes are excellent swimmers.

The smooth snake is a great rarity in Britain. Smooth snakes are widely distributed on the Open Forest and are found in mature stands of heather.

Left: The Forestry Commission's head keeper, Martin Noble, surveys for our rarest snakes.

Below: This carving of a snake catcher can be seen in the graveyard of St Nicholas Church in Brockenhurst. Harry 'Brusher' Mills was a professional snakecatcher.

Below left: Brusher Mills is still celebrated at The Snakecatcher pub near Brockenhurst Station.

Ponds

There are estimated to be about 300 larger ponds big enough to be mapped on the Open Forest. The special wildlife of some Forest ponds may be equally happy in a wheel rut or a mucky puddle which is flooded just for a few weeks a year.

On the Bramshaw Commons, ponds and ruts not much bigger than a washing up bowl provide a home for plants such as wild chamomile, pennyroyal mint and the small flea-bane. The fairy shrimp thrives in ponds which are dry most of the year and then when wet, the water is thick with cowpats and urine. The shrimps are able to hatch out and grow to be adults in a few short weeks when the pond is just right.

On the Beaulieu heaths, similar hollows created by tracks to the abandoned airfield support miniature gardens which include national rarities such as yellow century, chaff-weed and allseed. The special species of these seasonal ponds depend on the hard grazing, trampling and dunging of the commoners' animals. The New Forest is the major stronghold of many rare pond species which were once widespread in the commons and village greens of lowland Britain.

The bigger ponds on the Open Forest are nearly all man made. Hatchet Pond at Beaulieu and Eyeworth Pond by Fritham were built to provide power and water for industry. If you walk from Hatchet towards Lymington, the roadside is lined with ponds dug for gravel to repair the road, and at Crockford Bridge there are ponds which are the flooded remains of marl pits. Within these ponds and pools, many specialist plants thrive, including Hampshire purslane and the New Forest crowfoot, both species which rarely exist outside the Forest in Britain.

Above: *Burley Long Pond.*

Opposite: *Mogshade Pond.*

Whitten Pond.

Woods

The two dominant trees in Open Forest woods are oak and beech with holly growing beneath their shade. Within the woods there are a great variety of other trees including hazel, yew, rowan, whitebeam, ash and field maple and more rarely small leaved lime, elm and wild service. The New Forest is the largest area of native beech woodland in Britain.

Over the centuries the Open Forest woodlands have been modified by exploitation for fuelwood and for timber. The sheer size of the woodlands, at nearly 5000ha, and the long periods between times of heavy exploitation, have allowed the woods to retain many more natural features which most other woods in Britain have lost. The commoners' animals have free access and so maintain the tradition of having large grazing animals in woods.

Grazing helps maintain a structure of open sunny glades. These glades may be grasslands, or bogs or heaths. The clean air and abundant ancient trees mean that many specialist species associated with ancient woods are found in the Forest. There are particularly spectacular mushrooms and toadstools, as well as a great diversity of fungi, lichens, liverworts and mosses.

A mare and foal in a woodland glade.

Fungi of Forest glades and woods.

Above: *The tiny wood cricket brings the dry Forest floor alive with singing through the hot summer months.*

Right: *Mosses and leaves on the shady Forest floor.*

Below: *Honey buzzards feed on grubs in the woodland, nests of wasps, hornets and bees.*

Opposite: *The lumbering flight of stag beetles can be seen around Forest villages on still summer evenings.*

The Open Forest woods on the Crown land are locally called 'Ancient and Ornamental Woods' or 'A&O' as this is what they were called in the 1877 New Forest Act. There are areas of A&O woods within some forestry plantations and these are called pre-inclosure woods.

In many areas the woodland floor is carpeted with fallen leaves and mosses. The moss flora is diverse and beautiful and includes many rare species. The woods of the Open Forest have an undeserved reputation of being poor for wild flowers. In the scrubs around glades and in woodlands with richer soils, the show of springtime flowers can be very impressive. Grazing by Forest animals means that most plants are rather small, so although there is a great deal to be seen and enjoyed, you do have to make an effort to see it.

Forest woods often have many dead trees. When a tree dies it creates a whole set of habitats. Dead trees provide food and a home for a great variety of insects. One of Britain's largest insects is the stag beetle and the Forest has been identified as being of international importance for this creature. Recent studies are now suggesting that the stag beetle may live in the Forest but they seem to prefer the gardens of Forest villages and of neighbouring towns.

Heaps of deadwood from fallen trees provide tangles of branches and a place for scrub and brambles. These tangles protect the wild grown seedlings and saplings of the next generation of trees from being eaten. There was a time when people were worried about the lack of young trees in Open Forest woods. We now realise that if we leave dead wood to naturally rot away, it helps secure the natural regeneration of the woodland.

Over the centuries the wild mammals of the Forest's woods have changed. Our native wild species of deer now roam with deer introduced from other parts of the world. Native wild boar and beaver disappeared hundreds of years ago and wild ponies and cattle thousands of years ago. In the last fifty years, the native red squirrel have been replaced by grey squirrels. Otters and water voles hold on as small populations but they now share their rivers with American mink. The bats of the Forest remain diverse. In recent years studies have revealed at least 12 species of bat on the Open Forest including Bechsteins and barbestelles, both creatures of our largest and most ancient woods. Greater horseshoe bats still live in the Forest in a single cellar on the edge of the Avon Valley.

Right: *Pipistrelles and many other bats will roost in hollow trees.*

Opposite: *The fallen ancient tree provides shelter for the saplings of the next generation.*

As the Forest is a wet place you don't have to travel far to come across a river. Most of the rivers are small; there are few so large that you cannot wade across and many so small you can jump over them.

The largest of the Open Forest rivers is one of the least seen. The Beaulieu River rises near the police station at Lyndhurst and joins the salt water of the estuary at Beaulieu mill pond. For much of its course the Beaulieu River runs through woodlands, including some of the best flood plain forests in Europe. In a wet winter, the whole woodland can become flooded to over a metre deep, with the river flowing through a maze of channels between the trees.

Where the river is shaded it has few water plants, most of the energy for the abundant river life coming from the breakdown of dead wood and leaves. When the river flows through sunny glades and lawns there is a colourful show of water crowfoots and water lilies and the air is full of dragonflies. In the slightly salty waters of the Beaulieu mill pond the grazed muddy shallows are home to one of England's rarest, and least dramatic, plants, the dwarf spike-rush.

Right: *Beaulieu mill pond is slightly salty; here the Solent's tidal waters meet the Forest.*

Opposite: *The Highland Water is one of the tributaries of the Lymington River. Each part of the Lymington River has a different name.*

The rivers support fine runs of sea trout, but it is the modest bullhead and the river lamprey which bring a European importance to the Forest's river wildlife. These fish are dependant on the high quality of the water and the naturalness of the riverbed which are used by scientists throughout Europe to identify important rivers. The lamprey is a curious jawless fish, sometimes no bigger than a large earthworm, which spawns in the shallow gravel beds of quiet stretches of river. If you pick up a lamprey you can feel the tiny teeth which line its sucker working away at your skin.

The rivers of the north of the Forest are much smaller than those which flow into the Solent. The northern rivers are tributaries of the River Test and River Avon, with the Dockens Water recognised as a part of the internationally-important Avon river system. None of the Forest's rivers have entirely escaped the attention of drainage engineers. However compared to nearly every other river in the country, and most rivers in lowland western Europe, the Forest rivers are as natural as you can get. Natural rivers are rarely the same from one year to the next; the river changes its course, shallows and deeps move and the meanders coil across the floodplains.

Above: *The Avon Water flows through the Forest and out to sea at Keyhaven.*

Right: *Mandarin ducks escaped from wildfowl collections and have been breeding along wooded rivers in the Forest since the 1980s.*

DISCOVERING THE OPEN FOREST WITH A MAP

For 200 years, the New Forest has been mapped by the Ordnance Survey at nearby Southampton, which has recorded some of the place-names on the Open Forest. As there are seldom clear boundaries in the Open Forest, place-names are rather different from those on a street map or a landscape of fields. Names belong to a general area rather than a fixed point. Forest placenames are gradually changing, with some being lost from common use and new names emerging. By reading the map, and by understanding the placenames, a walk can become an exploration of the Forest's history and way of life.

Legal Differences in a Landscape

A map of the Open Forest reveals clues as to how parts of it are different from one another. Place-names help to reveal the historic and sometimes current legal status of the land.

The Bishop's Dyke near Beaulieu Road Station.

There are many purlieus shown on the maps, mostly around the edge of the Open Forest. A 'purlieu' is an area of Open Forest which may look the same as the Forest but which had been freed from forest law in the Middle Ages. The Bishop of Winchester's Purlieu near Beaulieu Road Station is clearly marked from the Forest by a large earthwork called the Bishop's Dyke. There are other purlieus at Hale, Brune's and Ogdens in the north of the Forest. Brune's Purlieu is partially heathland but is no longer a part of the Open Forest. Dibden Purlieu near Hythe is now part of the towns of the Waterside. The word purlieu has no practical meaning in the modern administration of the Forest.

Cattle on Half Moon Common.

St Peter's Church at Bramshaw.

The place-name 'common' is usually applied to a privately owned part of the Open Forest. The Bramshaw Commons only really became part of the New Forest in 1964 and even now there are some subtle differences in administration. These commons include Half Moon Common, Cadnam Common, Penn Common, Wellow and Plaitford Commons. The Bramshaw Commons were historically part of the Royal Forests of Melchet and Clarendon in Wiltshire. These commons are sometimes called the northern commons. There is another series of commons on the west of the Forest including Ibsley, Hyde, Gorley and Rockford Commons.

The Half-and-half Church

St Peter's Church at Bramshaw sits on a hill which until 1894 marked the boundary between Hampshire and Wiltshire. The hill has also marked the boundary between the New Forest and the Forests of Melchet and Clarendon. The shape of the hill meant that the church had to grow in width rather than in length. Tradition has it that half the church used to be in Hampshire and the other half in Wiltshire.

On the Crown land the word common is rarely used. On rare occasions such as at Blackfield Common near Fawley the place-name reflects historic disputes between the Crown and neighbouring manors.

The place-names of the Crown land on the Open Forest usually describe something in the landscape rather than the administrative status of the land.

Place-names on the Open Forest and their Meaning

Balls

In the northwest of the Forest the hills are called 'balls' such as Burnt Balls by Long Bottom near Blissford, and Sandy Balls.

Burnt Balls.

Bogs

Bogs are very wet peaty places difficult to cross on foot. In recent years the more scientific word 'mires' has become used to describe Forest bogs. The name bog is only occasionally shown on a map, such as at Hinchelsea Bog near Brockenhurst, but the word is regularly used when the management of the Forest is discussed.

Bottoms

Bottom, meaning a valley, is one of the most commonly-mapped place-names and is found throughout the Forest. The valley may contain other features such as bogs, gutters or lawns. Bottoms provide opportunities for schoolboy humour with entertaining destinations for walks such as Broad Bottom and Slap Bottom by Burley.

Down

Downs are areas of open heathland. They are often a high place with extensive views such as Acres Down near Emery Down or Black Down near Beaulieu Road.

Slap Bottom at Burley.

Driftways or Droves

These are unfenced routes for Forest animals through fenced landscapes such as the plantations south of Lyndhurst or the lanes to the Avon Valley north of

Ringwood. These routes are still used for driving animals from one part of the Open Forest to another. A driftway is usually the most interesting walking route through a block of plantations.

Furze or Furzey

Furze, sometimes pronounced 'fuzz', refers to an area with a lot of gorse, such as Gurnetfields Furzebrake near Beaulieu. These can be very difficult to walk through particularly where the gorse is old and tall.

Fern or Ferny

Fern refers to bracken stands. These are often on the drier parts of the Open Forest in places such as Ferny Knap near Rhinefield.

Garns

Garns are historic locations for groups of beehives to be set out on the heath, such as at Hive Garn Bottom near Godshill.

Above: *There is a long tradition of bee keeping on the Forest.*

Right: *Hatchet Pond where the Forest gate leads to the Beaulieu estate.*

Below: *Swan Green.*

Gate

An entrance to the Crown land, such as at Gatewood Hill near Langley or Moonshill Gate at Beaulieu. The word 'Hatch' is used in other royal forests in England to mean the entrance to the forest and may be the origin of New Forest place-names Hatchet Green on the northern boundary of the Forest, and Hatchet Gate by Beaulieu.

Green

A grassy area. Greens can be next to villages, such as Swan Green at Lyndhurst, or deep in the Forest such as Camel Green at Gritnam. Where greens are next to villages they are sometimes called settlement edge lawns.

Gutter

A small river, often running in a deep slot cut into soft soils, such as Black Gutter under Deadman's Hill near Godshill or Shepherd's Gutter near Bramshaw.

Hat

A small wood standing on its own, often on a high place, such as Great Hat at Holmsley. Some hats, such as Little Stubby Hat near Cadnam are now part of much larger woods. Hats such as Cardinal's Hat at Holmsley are currently within inclosures.

Heath

Heath is a very common place-name. A heath is much more than a landscape dominated by heathers. A heath is a mixture of heather, furze brakes, holms, hats, bottoms, ponds, lawns and many other features.

Left: *The heaths of Rockford and Ibsley Commons.*

Below: *Balmer Lawn; a landscape of mounds formed by grasses trapping silt from winter floods.*

Holms

A holm is a wood of holly trees, such as at Holmsley or Holm Hill near Rhinefield. A holm may also be a hat.

Lawn

A grassy area much prized by commoners as the best grazing. Lawns may be found where winter flooding enriches the soil, such as Balmer Lawn near Brockenhurst or as Forest glades such as Wide Lawn near Gritnam. Lawns are also often found next to villages or near isolated Forest farms. These lawns are maintained by the animals belonging to the people who turn them out. Year-round hard grazing can create a lawn out of a heathland.

Lodge

The place name lodge appears several times on the Open Forest. Lodges were houses, often with fields, associated with the management of the Forest. In places such as The Churchyard, west of Fritham, or Queen's Bower near Brockenhurst, there are lodges which have been abandoned and returned to the Open Forest. Elsewhere in the Forest, lodges and their fields survive as homes and farms, such as Burley Lodge and Ashurst Lodge.

Moor

Moor is the historic name for a bog such as at Cranesmoor and Vales Moor near Burley. As bogs are found throughout the Forest heaths, the place-name moor on a map does not always pin-point the bog.

Park

The Ordnance Survey map of the Forest shows a Park Pale running across the heaths south of Boltons Bench at Lyndhurst. This is the historic boundary of Lyndhurst Park, an area divided by a paling fence from the rest of the Forest in the medieval period to allow for the King's deer to be managed separately from commoners' animals. Lyndhurst Park is now partially Open Forest, part inclosure and partially private grounds. Other ancient Parks, such as New Park and Brockenhurst Park, are private and are firmly fenced from the Open Forest.

Passage

A passage is a safe route across a bog such as at Woodfidley Passage and Matley Passage, both near Denny.

The passage across Harvest Slade.

Plain

A plain is a large area of open flat land, very often on a high place such as Fritham Plain and Ocknell Plain in the north of the Forest.

Pound

When walking the Forest you will encounter stout wooden corrals. These are the pounds which temporarily hold Forest animals when they have been rounded up on a drift. The pounds are shown on some maps as well as in place-names such as Poundhill Heath, north of Brockenhurst.

Turf Hill Pound.

Rocks

The Forest is mostly made up of clay and gravel soils. Very locally, particularly around Burley, the presence of outcrops of iron-rich sandrocks are commemorated in place names such as Burley Rocks and Rock Hills.

Reseed

The reseeds are areas of heathland and natural grassland that were ploughed up as part of the 'Dig for Victory' campaign in the 1940s. The reseeds are now grasslands and have become colonised with Forest wildlife. These areas often appear on maps not as place-name but a curious dotted line around a rather featureless bit of Open Forest, such as at Long Slade Bottom north of Sway.

Shade

A shade is where Forest animals will stand and rest, such as Mogshade. These are usually places such as breezy hill tops where the biting flies are scarce. A shade may be a place in full sunlight.

Shute or Shoot

A path down a steep hillside, such as at Redshoot.

Slades

Slades are broad valleys. This place-name is most common in the centre of the Forest in places such as Warwick Slade and Harvest Slade between Burley and Lyndhurst.

Harvest Slade.

Trench

Salisbury Trench, on the road between Bramshaw and Godshill records the historic clearing back of woodlands to deter highway robbery. The Trench is still kept clear of dense shrub cover, no longer to deter highwaymen but to help prevent traffic accidents between motorists and Forest animals.

Wood

On the Open Forest the place-name wood is usually associated with one of the natural woodlands grazed by Forest animals. Some of the larger woods are Bramshaw Great Wood, Busketts Wood near Ashurst and Frame Wood near Beaulieu. Grazing means that few branches grow within reach of the mouths of cattle, ponies and deer. The height to which animals can reach is called the browse line. To the walker, the browse line allows you to walk freely through the wood without dense areas of shrubs to block your way. This is reflected in the place-name Browse Wood near Nomansland.

EIGHT

THE NATIONAL PARK COAST

The National Park coast runs from under the shadow of the power station at the Jolly Sailor pub at Ashlett round to The Gun pub at Keyhaven at the foot of Hurst Spit.

The Forest has a soft, sheltered coast; a place of mud and gravel. Tidal rivers, wooded shores and marshes cut into the broad sweep of the western Solent. This coastline looks out onto land and not to the open sea. The Isle of Wight and the eastern shores of Southampton Water provide a constant backdrop.

The shoreline is not a remote place; fine houses have been built in the farmland and woods which run down to the high tide mark. Offshore, the water is always busy with vessels from the great ports of Southampton and Portsmouth and from fleets of yachts and pleasure boats. The beauty of the coast is appreciated by those who like low horizons and distant views.

Why is the New Forest Coast special?

The Jolly Sailor at Ashlett Creek. A gateway to the National Park coast.

It is convenient but artificial to separate a description of the coast from the Open Forest. Historically much of the Forest's coast was part of the Open Forest. A combination of the fencing of the perambulation in the 1960s and the more recent fencing of the coast in private estates has reduced, but not cut, the connection. The Open Forest still meets the tidal waters of the Solent at Beaulieu mill pond and on the Boldre foreshore. Forest commoners turn out their animals to graze Ashlett Green and the marshes in front of the power station. The nature reserve grazing marshes west of Lymington are also grazed by Forest commoners. The coast is special as a part of the Open Forest landscape and the heritage of Forest commoning.

The great bulk of Hurst Castle dominates the entrance to the western Solent.

The Isle of Wight is the backdrop to the Open Forest along the Boldre foreshore.

The coast of the Forest is also part of the much larger coastal wetlands of the Solent. The Solent is one of the richest coastal wetlands of north west Europe for its wildlife and of exceptional importance for its great diversity of habitats and the many rare species these support. In winter, huge numbers of birds travel vast distances from the Arctic tundra and from northern Europe to feed in the wetlands of the Solent. In summer the wilder open spaces support important colonies of breeding birds.

The natural beauty of the Forest's coast has long been recognised as of national importance. The beauty comes from the mixture of naturalness combined with a landscape rich in monuments from a history of industry and warfare.

Compared to many other rural coastlines in England, the New Forest coast is a busy place. When compared to many other parts of South East England, the Forest's coast is relatively undeveloped for housing and industry, but heavily developed for recreation.

In that division of New Forest which is confined by Beaulieu River and the bay of Southampton both the river and the bay, are woody, and full of beautiful scenery.

Sowley Pond; once the energy source for an iron works.

Bucklers Hard; a village designed to service shipyards.

The Industrial Coast

William Gilpin wrote about the beauty of the Forest's coast in his 'Remarks on Forest Scenery' over 200 years ago. When Gilpin lived in the Forest, the coast was a place of industry. At Sowley Pond, west of Beaulieu, are the remains of the freshwater lake that drove the watermill for an iron foundry which produced cannon and shot for the Royal Navy and the East India Company. Attempts were made to ship iron ore from the north of England to use the water power of Sowley Pond and the abundant fuel provided by the charcoal industry around the Forest. Once the coal fields and iron-works in the north of England grew, then iron working was no longer profitable in the Forest and was abandoned .

Most of the major villages in the Forest have ancient origins. Surveys such as the Doomsday book describe the manors and farmsteads that have grown to become the villages of today. Buckler's Hard on the Beaulieu River is different.

Buckler's Hard was created in the early 1720s with the idea that it would become a major port. At that time there were high profits to be made from sugar grown on the islands of the Caribbean. The Duke of Montagu planned to establish plantations on St Vincent and St Lucia and import sugar into his new port on the Beaulieu River, which was to be called Montagu Town.

The Duke gained permission from Parliament to colonise the islands and in 1722, at his own expense sent a fleet of seven ships to the Caribbean. The islanders did not welcome the Duke's men and with the help of the French defeated the colonists. Montagu Town failed as a port for the sugar trade but the ground was ready for the re-named Buckler's Hard to emerge as one of the great ship-building yards of England.

By the end of the century, Britain's empire and political stability was threatened by the American War of Independence, the French Revolution and the rise of Napoleon. War gave new purpose to Buckler's Hard, and the village grew up to take advantage of contracts to build ships for the Royal Navy. A broad central street lined with houses, timber yards and chandlers ran down to slipways and moorings on the tidal Beaulieu River. Buckler's Hard was one of a number of private shipyards around the Solent drawing on the timber reserves of the Crown lands of the Forest and the neighbouring landed estates.

In what appears a small village, some of the largest warships of the age were built at Buckler's Hard. The most celebrated was HMS *Agamemnon*, a ship with 62 guns, a 49-metre long gun deck and a crew of over 500. The ship took four years to build and was launched in 1781 to serve against the French in the Caribbean. Nelson commanded the ship for three years and he described her as 'the finest ship I ever sailed in'. The history of the people and the shipyards is told in the Maritime Museum at Buckler's Hard.

The wooden walls of England of Nelson's Navy gave way to iron clads and Buckler's Hard lost the trade of building warships. The ship-building tradition is not entirely lost. The Agamemnon Yard is now home to a company building motor yachts.

Civilian industries were also found along the coast and have also left their mark. The abundance of the charcoal which fuelled the iron works were also used by brickworks and saltworks. Scattered among the mudlands of the Beaulieu River and the Boldre foreshore are thousands of waste bricks and tiles. The New Forest brickworks were able to use a variety of local clays and produced fashionable 'white' bricks as well as traditional redbrick.

The scattered houses at Pitts Deep are all that remain of a once busy wharf serving the heavy industries of this part of the Forest. Brick making survived in the Forest until living memory but with the coming of the railways, the brickyards moved away from the coast towards an easy supply of coal and to the growing railway towns.

Salt making was particularly well developed around Lymington. The modern coastal landscape between Lymington and Keyhaven is dominated by the remains of this industry. It is not known when salt making in the Solent started. In other estuaries in England, archaeologists have discovered saltworks from before the Roman invasion. The New Forest salt industry probably has similar ancient origins.

In the late seventeenth century, the Lymington saltworks were visited by Celia Fiennes. Fiennes took an interest in everything in her travels but may have been particularly interested in salt working as she owned property in Cheshire where rock salt was mined. She described how although Lymington had a few ships in the harbour, its greatest trade was making salt.

In spring sea water was drawn into trenches and ponds created along the edge of the marshes. Over the following months the sea water was gradually concentrated by allowing the summer sun to evaporate off the water. The water was moved from pond to pond until it was concentrated enough for the brine to be boiled in large square iron and copper pans. The hot thick salty mass was then packed into great baskets where the remaining water would run off to leave blocks of salt. The smoke for the salthouse fires and the windmills which pumped the salt water have both disappeared. Low mounds in the marsh hint at the location of where the brine was boiled and the salt was stored. A few buildings from this great industry survive such as the barns at Moses Dock on the Keyhaven coastal path.

Moses Dock.

A walk along the lanes and sea walls between the Chequers Pub west of Lymington and The Gun pub in Keyhaven takes you through a landscape of pools and earthworks. These are the remains of the salt industry which had fallen into decay by the 1860s and been taken over by more modern uses. One of the salt ponds, Eight Acre Pond, was used as a shellfish farm before it became part of a nature reserve and a safe training ground for sailing. Most of the remains of the saltworks are now part of the grazing marshes of Hampshire County Council's Keyhaven and Pennington nature reserve.

The twice daily tides provided reliable energy for watermills all along the coast. Tide mills could be driven both by the tide and by trapping lakes of sea water at high tide for release later. Within the National Park there are historic tide mill buildings at Ashlett Creek and on the Beaulieu mill pond. Just outside the Park boundary, at Eling Creek, the tide mill still works, grinding corn using the same sustainable power source as it has for hundreds of years.

The marshes and lagoons of Pennington.

Above: *Ashlett Tide Mill: now a social club for the Oil Refinery.*

Left: *Looking across Beaulieu mill pond to Palace House.*

The main industry on the Forest's coast today is agriculture. Most of the coast is farmed by the five landed estates which own much of the countryside along the shore. In some areas such as along the Beaulieu River, at Keyhaven, Calshot, Lepe and Lymington recreation, tourism and leisure is now a big business.

Yachts at Lymington.

Tourism on the Forest's coast has a long history. William Gilpin was encouraging visitors to enjoy the beauty of the Forest's coast over 200 years ago. Before the coming of the railway, access to the coast from Portsmouth and Southampton was difficult overland but easy by sea. History records Jane Austen as having taken a boat trip to the Beaulieu River, but unfortunately does not record her impressions.

In 1894 a steam launch began a service running from Gosport to Bucklers Hard at a price where the workers of the growing cities of Hampshire's industrial coast could enjoy the beauty of the western Solent. Today tourism is based on private cars bringing with it all of the benefits and problems of traffic. The sounds of the hammers of the iron works and shipyards and the fumes from salt houses and brick kilns have been replaced by those of the internal combustion engine.

The Military Coast

The National Park coast is part of one of Britain's busiest military coastlines. The sheltered harbours of the Solent are the home of the British Navy and have been the backdrop of numerous invasions. The Forest coast forms part of the western approaches to the Solent as well as the entrance to Southampton Water.

On the road into the Forest out of Lymington are the Buckland Rings. From the road Buckland Rings looks like a low wooded hill. A short walk along the footpaths reveal huge earthworks rising above the surrounding land. Buckland Rings are one of the many Iron Age hillforts of the New Forest. Hill forts are thought not only to have been built for defence in time of war, but also to have been the centre of some Iron Age communities. Modern industry and houses hide how close Buckland Rings are to the Lymington River and to its tributary, the Passford Water. At the time the fort was built, over 2500 years ago, the river was an arm of the sea and an important gateway to the coast and to the Forest.

Buckland Rings: a gateway to the National Park from Lymington.

Much more recently in the 1540s Henry VIII had castles built on the shingle spits of Hurst and Calshot. Fearing invasion from the French and the Spanish, the King fortified the entrances to the western Solent and the mouth of Southampton Water. A few years earlier the King had broken the power of the monasteries. The monks of Beaulieu Abbey had been driven away and their buildings confiscated. The great Abbey Church and its many outbuildings were taken apart to provide the building stone for Hurst and Calshot castles.

When Calshot Castle was built it sat on the end on a long spit in the same way that Hurst Castle does today. After the Second World War, the marshes of this part of

Southampton Water were built up to create land for industry. The power station was built on part of the new shoreline and the remainder is the wild open space called Tom Tiddler's Ground.

Calshot Castle now stands on the stump of its spit, dwarfed by giant barn-like buildings of a modern recreation centre. These were formerly aircraft hangers, built in the First World War at a time when large aircraft were designed to take off from calm coastal waters rather than concrete runways. The Calshot hangers were once home to flying boats such as the Shorts Sunderland and the early seaplane versions of the Supermarine Spitfire.

The hangers at Calshot are the remains of an airport for sea planes.

As Calshot guarded Southampton Water so Hurst Castle protected the Solent's western approaches. The Tudor castle is still intact and for a while was the prison of King Charles I on his final journey to trial and execution. The Tudor castle was greatly expanded by Victorian engineers, and some of the giant guns that were housed in the fort are on display. The castle is open to visitors over the summer months and is accessible by a bracing walk along the spit from Milford or by the passenger ferry from Keyhaven. This is an excellent introduction to the coast of the National Park.

Hurst Spit from the air. Every year the spit changes shape.

The boundary of the National Park forms a line which cuts across the wetlands of the western Solent. The Solent rarely freezes for long in winter and is a rich source of food making it ideal as the winter home for over 50,000 estuary birds. These birds come to the Solent from as far away as northern Europe, western Siberia, Iceland and parts of the Canadian Arctic. Some birds spend the whole winter in the Solent, others rely on its abundant food to help them on longer journeys. The Solent is one of the largest of a series of estuaries which fall within the migration path of nearly 10 million wading birds, 8 million ducks and 700,000 geese and swans.

Hundreds of wigeon feed on the eelgrass meadows before moving onto the coastal marshes.

Ringed plovers visiting the Solent travel as far afield as Ghana, Greenland and Poland.

Above: *Curlew nest on the Open Forest. In winter up to a thousand curlew feed in the more sheltered estuaries.*

Above left: *Over 2000 brent geese may arrive on the Lymington Marshes from Taymyr in western Siberia.*

Left: *At high tide brent geese feed on farmland along the Forest's coast.*

Mud covered by sea water on the highest tides can become colonised by plants which can survive both salt water and being regularly drowned. These plants can stabilise the mud to create saltmarsh. The first plants to get a foothold in the mud are the glassworts. There are six species of glassworts on the Forest coast, some growing on the mud as brilliant green glass pencils while others are more like branched candlesticks. The flowers are almost invisible to the human eye as they are hidden within knee-like scales on the smooth stems.

The Solent saltmarshes are known throughout the world for salt tolerant grasses called cord-grass. It was in Southampton Water that during the nineteenth century that an American species of cord-grass was accidentally introduced. The pollen of this grass mixed with the British native cord-grass and eventually produced two new species, Townsend's cord-grass and common cord-grass. These new species both were first found in the grazed salt marshes of the Open Forest.

For fifty years cord grass marshes spread out over mudflats throughout the western Solent. The grass is now dying back and marshes are turning into mudflats.

The new species of cord-grasses were incredibly successful and colonised a large area of coastal mud, first around the Solent and then elsewhere in Britain and around the world. The habitats of mudflats and eelgrass meadows rapidly changed to saltmarsh as the cord-grass spread. In the Solent the cord-grass marshes reached their greatest extent in the 1920s and are now dying back. As the cord-grass dies, so the saltmarshes that it helped to create are turning back into mudflats.

In summer the undisturbed saltmarshes provide a safe nesting place for birds which breed on the ground. Over the last hundred years, the saltmarshes have become colonised by birds such as redshank and black headed gulls. These birds need to be free from disturbance and predators and so live in wide open spaces. As our country-side has changed so the coast has become more important to them. It is possible to enjoy the spectacle of the huge flocks of black headed gulls which nest on the Boldre foreshore from the deck of the Lymington Ferry. In the many nature reserves which line the coast, there are colonies of four species of terns as well as the occasional pair of Mediterranean gulls, a recent arrival on the Forest coast.

The beaches of the Forest coast are also important breeding bird habitats. Oystercatchers, terns, ringed plovers and shelduck all nest on the ground near the shore. These birds cannot survive disturbance and are now almost only found in the sanctuary of nature reserves. Plants grow in the sand and shingle among the nests away from the pressure of trampling human feet.

A common tern and sea purslane.

Flowers of the shingle shore: thrift and sea campion

Yellow horned poppy.

The coastline of today has been influenced by hundred of years of engineering. Sea walls have been built around marshes and barriers have been put across rivers to stop salt water moving upstream. Behind the seawalls of the marshes between Lymington and Keyhaven there are salt marshes and salt meadows lying below sea level.

In among the grasslands are salt water lagoons. The lagoons of the western Solent support some of Britain's rarest wildlife. Only the most specialised plants and animals can live in ponds that can quickly change from being slightly salty to being much saltier than the sea. The wildlife that can cope with these extremes include tasselweed together with the foxtail stonewort, which is a curious seaweed which builds itself a skeleton of calcium. The creatures of the lagoons include the insensible shrimp, the lagoon sand worm and the Isle of Wight starlet anemone, so called because scientists first discovered it at Bembridge on the Island.

In many places the coast gradually changes into dry land. In the sheltered waters of the Beaulieu River reedbeds grow under the ancient woods which reach down to the tidal muds. In among the reeds may be found the two-metre high dandylion-like marsh sow thistle. Reedbeds are scattered along the coast, the largest being on the Lymington River. This reedbed grew up within living memory after the grazing marshes of the Lymington were abandoned. Sea level rise now means the reedbeds are becoming a shallow brackish lake with swamps as the river water has difficulty escaping to the sea.

The Lymington River reedbeds.

All of the wildlife of the Solent is special. What makes the Forest's coast particularly important is that the habitats all join up with one another and change with time and the tides. The coast joins with the Open Forest and with the Forest's countryside to provide one of the richest and most varied coastlines in Britain's National Parks.

THE NATIONAL PARK COUNTRYSIDE

It is not easy to discover the Forest's countryside as most of the farmland in the National Park is private land and the number of footpaths and public places are limited. There are large country estates which own parts of the Park and there is an increasing number of small landowners who own just a few acres. In the past those who studied the Forest have been drawn to the Open Forest and the coast. A great deal of work has yet to be done to fully understand the land within fields and fences. From what we already know the countryside of the Forest is an important part of the landscapes that collectively make up the National Park.

Opposite and below: *Growing straw for thatching in countryside to the west of the Forest.*

At first sight there are areas of countryside in the National Park that look rather unremarkable. In many parishes, farming is being replaced by leisure and so fields that were once cropped for hay or oats now are home to riding horses, trailers, sheds and assorted clutter. Gardens are creeping into the neighbouring paddocks with exotic trees, toys and security lights. It is sometimes difficult to tell what is countryside and what is not. Within this muddle there are intriguing places that rightfully earn the Forest's countryside its place in the National Park.

In among the horse paddocks and extended gardens of the fashionable and wealthy, the commoners may have their holdings. These are the lands that bring with them the ancient common rights. These are the places where hay is grown for winter feed and the Forest animals live when they are not roaming free. A few commoners are fortunate in having land that they own themselves. Agricultural land prices in the Forest can be up to nearly eight times the average price of farmland in England, so many commoners rent land rather than buy it. The fields of the Forest's countryside support the commoners who care for the animals which are the architects of the Forest.

In the same way as the countryside has a relationship with the people of the Open Forest, so it is with wildlife. The nightjars which nest out on the heath are known to fly many kilometres to find food. The private woods near the heaths have a rich insect life and help feed the young nightjars. A curlew which nests on the heath in summer may spend winter out on the salt marshes of the coast and also feed in the rich wet pastures of cattle fields. When Montague's harriers recently nested on the Forest, the adults hunted the quiet private meadows of the Avon Valley. Wildlife does not recognise the boundaries that we put on a landscape.

The wildlife of the coast also uses the Forest's countryside. At high tide the flocks of wintering birds are driven off the mud and marshes and move inland to rest and feed on the larger grassland fields. Rabbit holes in dry sandy hedgebanks by the coast double as the nests of shelduck. When the ducklings are ready the adult birds march them down to the shore.

Even unremarkable small fields can be valuable to coastal birds. After the hay crop is safely stored and the late summer ponies are taken into dry winter quarters, a small paddock can be home to green sandpipers, egrets, heron, flocks of gulls and the occasional curlew. If there is food and the birds feel safe from predators and disturbance, even an ordinary paddock may play its part in providing a place for nature.

Many of the farms and woods in the countryside have been cut out of the Open Forest at some time in history. There are ancient oaks in fields and on hedge banks which will have grown up and been in their prime when the farm did not exist and the young tree was a part of a wilder landscape. Bits of the Open Forest have survived the planting of hedges and there are some farms that are mixtures of heathy grasslands with swathes of purple moor grass, gorse and heathers. Some wet fields contain bogs that were hedged out of the Open Forest maybe hundreds of years ago but still are wet and peaty.

There are probably hundreds of meadows which are dominated by wild grasses and flowers such as fescue grasses, red clover, and oxeye daisies. These are simple, pretty places that are becoming increasingly rare elsewhere in England. Remains of ancient wood pastures can be found in the larger woods. These relics of former wooded commons still may be grazed in the woody corners of a farm. The special places of the Forest's countryside are still being discovered, and we still do not really understand all that is out there.

Even where the countryside has become tatty and forlorn, the very pattern of the land can tell the history of the Forest. Each farm, each field, was made by someone at some time. The Forest is special in that the landscape and historic documents combine to show how farms have been created from the Forest for over a thousand years. The pattern of fields tells the story of people in the Forest that is far older than any building.

There are many places in the Forest's countryside where people are welcome to discover for themselves what makes it special.

Avon Valley

The River Avon is one of the grander rivers of England. At Salisbury, the many chalk streams of the upper Avon join together to form one large river flowing in a broad grassy valley to the sea at Christchurch.

The view from Castle Hill, near Woodgreen.

Four great bends in the river run through the National Park. This is the landscape of meadows and water between Charford on the Wiltshire border and Burgate by Fordingbridge. Here the National Park boundary follows the New Forest perambulation of 1278. The landmarks on Kings Edward's boundary of Breamore Mill and the Charford Farms are still there today.

Latchmoor Brook is a tributary of the Avon.

The Avon Valley is another of the many parts of the National Park recognised as having international importance for wildlife. It is the river itself that is special. Along the western edge of the Park the gin-clear waters of the Avon mix with sherry-tinted Forest streams. The small Forest streams have beds of clean gravels and fine silts. These are the breeding grounds of an exceptionally diverse range of fish including our native salmon, bullheads and the jawless sea and brook lampreys. In all 24 species of fish are known from the Avon.

The reedy fens by the river are home to Desmoulin's whorl snail. This is a rather small, inconspicuous creature but it is used by scientists to describe European importance for wildlife as it can only survive in the highest quality habitats. The plant life of the river is equally exceptional, with over 60 species of aquatic plant growing in the river and its side channels.

From the many bridges you can look down through the clear waters at ever-changing shapes as submerged plants are swept by the current. After the winter floods the plants grow rapidly up from the riverbed to hold their flowers clear of the water. In early summer the surface of the Avon can turn white with tens of thousands of crowfoot flowers.

A good place to start discovering the Avon Valley is from the top of Castle Hill outside the village of Woodgreen. Castle Hill is part of the Open Forest and ponies graze through the wooded cliff that drops 30 metres from the hilltop straight into the river. The view from Castle Hill takes in the broad lush meadows of the valley and beyond into the chalk hills of Wiltshire. Another vantage point looking over the valley is from the footpaths around the Iron Age hillfort of Frankenbury. The ramparts of the fort stand among the beechwoods which run down to the watermeadows below Sandy Balls.

The village hall at Woodgreen is decorated by a series of murals, painted in 1930 by Robert Baker and Edward Payner, which celebrate the view from Castle Hill and everyday events in village life.

The first impression from the hills is that the Avon Valley is broad and flat. A short walk along the footpaths reveals a much richer picture. The farms which line the valley are on slightly higher ground than their meadows. The winter floods rarely reach these ancient settlements.

Below the farms are meadows where the footpaths cross many small streams and overlook impressive earthworks, bridges and ironwork. These are the remains of a system of grassland farming which flourished in the valley from about 300 years ago. These fields are called water meadows, or floated meadows. The river was diverted through a series of artificial channels, banks and drains to water the grass, and the fields were engineered to make the most of the warm fertile water of the river.

Above left: Woodgreen Village Hall is decorated inside and out.

Above: The entrance into the village hall is under the ladders of the apple pickers.

Left: St Mary's Church at Hale stands high above the floodplain.

With flowing water the grass started growing earlier in the year giving heavier crops. Constant management meant that the water was always flowing and it was not allowed to stand or stagnate. Water meadows are part of a farming system which provided early grazing and hay for the farm. The Avon Valley has long been used by New Forest farmers to fatten up cattle that have spent their early life on the heaths of the Open Forest.

In the twentieth century, water meadows declined in value as the labour to maintain them became expensive and fertility could be bought in a bag of chemicals. The tradition of floating meadows in the part of the valley within the National Park survived until about 1950. Just north of the Park boundary the tradition continues in the village of Woodford.

Above: *Burgate meadows with Sandy Balls and Frankenbury hillfort beyond.*

Right: *The Burgate suspension bridge; a gateway to the Avon Valley in the National Park.*

In the twenty-first century the water meadows are finding a new purpose. The wetlands created by water meadows have great potential as places for wildlife, for managing winter floods and as places of wild beauty. The meadows still produce high quality natural grasslands which are used for fattening animals raised both in the valley and on the Open Forest. Since the 1990s, the valley has been identified as an Environmentally Sensitive Area with special grants to help the farmers in the valley meet this potential.

Downstream of Fordingbridge, the National Park boundary runs alongside the valley but never quite makes it to the river itself. Between the floodplain and the rising ground of the Forest heaths there is an area of flat, open farmland. This farmland lies over deposits of fine sands and gravels which have been dug for housing and industry for over fifty years. The flooded gravel pits formed the Blashford Lakes.

Remembering Alice

The Alice Lisle pub is one of the gateways to the National Park near Ringwood. The pub is bounded by the Blashford Lakes and overlooks the lanes and greens of the Open Forest. The pub commemorates Alice Lisle of nearby Moyles Court. In 1685 the Duke of Monmouth invaded England seeking the throne from King James II. Monmouth was defeated at the Battle of Sedgemoor and his followers became outlaws. Alice Lisle sheltered John Hickes and Richard Neilthorpe who had supported Monmouth. For this crime she was sentenced to death by being burnt alive. The King changed the sentence to death by beheading, and Alice Lisle was executed in Winchester Market Place in September 1685 at the age of seventy-one.

Left and above: *The Alice Lisle pub on Rockford Green.*

Below: *The Avon south of Fordingbridge, in full flood.*

The National Park boundary skirts around the Blashford Lakes and dips back down towards the river at Bisterne, south of Ringwood. Here footpaths lead to the ancient river crossing of Watton's Ford.

On these sandy lands on the western borders of the National Park, the poor soils support an almost desert-like dry, grassy heath. Winter winds whip up the fine sands which drop in the shelter of rough grasses or a hedge bank. In cold winters the crests of snow drifts can be crowned with lines of sand which fall to the ground as the snow melts to form tiny dunes.

These hungry, mobile soils are home to plants such as sand sedge, the tiny red succulent mossy stonecrop and many modest clovers. More stable areas develop a miniature landscape of branched lichens and dwarfed plants. Grass and lichen heaths are now very rare in the valley; they are fragile sensitive habitats and are found in farmland away from footpaths. One of the best areas of this landscape can be discovered a few hundred metres outside the National Park in the Blashford Lakes nature reserve, north of Ringwood.

Langley Woods

Great spotted woodpecker. The larger broadleaved woods of the Forest are home to all three species of our native woodpeckers.

The footpaths between the Wiltshire villages of Lover and Whiteparish run through the woodlands of the Langley Wood National Nature Reserve and Whiteparish Common. At first glance this looks like one large wood cut in two by the Salisbury Road, but as soon as you start to walk the paths it is clear that something special is inside. The public rights of way follow huge earthbanks, sometimes forming the sides of woodland lanes, and sometimes widening out to surround broad swathes of wood. These earthworks spread out from the lanes and criss-cross the wood. Some of these earthworks are as large as the pathside banks, others smaller and less clear. There are few truly ancient trees in the wood, but there are groves of old trees including giant coppice stools of small leaved limes.

The Langley Woods seem a long way from the Open Forest, but they are a part of the same historic and ecological landscape. The lanes running into Wiltshire from Hampshire were fenced from Forest animals within living memory. The great sweep of open heathland which used to run from Bramshaw Telegraph to the Langley Woods is now dominated by conifer plantations, farming and a large rubbish dump. The Wiltshire lanes still have the wide grassy verges and small roadside lawns typical of the Open Forest, but they are now ungrazed. It was only in the 1960s that cattle grazing finally stopped in the woods of Whiteparish Common and with it came the loss of its sunny glades full of wildflowers and butterflies.

The Langley Woods are a series of coppice woodlands which surrounded a part of the Open Forest called the Outwood. The Outwood is still named on the Ordnance Survey map which shows the wooded lanes and footpaths that lead into it. The Wiltshire part of today's New Forest was once part of the entirely different Clarendon and Melchet royal forests.

The Langley woods were never administered as part of the Open Forest. As the woods and commons were privately owned, the Langley Woods had their own officer, a Woodward, to make sure the woods were well managed and commoners did not abuse their grazing rights. The site of the abandoned Woodward's house and fields can be found in among the banks by the Outwood.

The Langley Woods are rich in woodland wildflowers. The best time of year to enjoy the flowers is in late spring before the trees come into full leaf.

Above left: *Primroses.*

Above: *Bluebells.*

Left: *Wood anemones.*

The earthworks which spread out from the Outwood can be explained by how the wood was grazed. The coppices that surrounded the Outwood were cut regularly to produce small wood. As soon as the wood was cut the coppices were protected from the grazing animals roaming in the Outwood by fences and earthbanks. However, when the cut trees had regrown to a height where the grazing animals could do no harm, the fences were taken down and the animals in the Outwood would again graze through the coppices.

Elsewhere around the Forest's countryside there are other large blocks of private woodlands with similar combinations of earthworks and connections with the historic Open Forest. What makes the Langley Woods particularly special is that historians and ecologists have been able to reveal the history of how people in the Forest have previously balanced the competing needs of wood production and food for grazing animals.

Fritham

The village of Fritham is an island of farmland surrounded by Open Forest. The island is almost round, as this is the most efficient way of enclosing the maximum area of farmland with the minimum length of hedge. Fritham is actually a carefully-planned ancient landscape.

The Royal Oak at Fritham, where the vaccary meets the Open Forest.

The farms of Fritham are formed from one of 10 farms created by Saxon Kings in the Forest. These farms were cut out of the open landscapes of the Forest and set up with tenants who would have paid their rent to the Crown in cheese. These farms are known as vaccaries from the Latin and French words for cow. In the same way that the deer on the Open Forest provided a living larder of fresh meat for the Crown, so the farms in the vaccaries provided a dairy.

The shape of the Saxon vaccary can been seen from the roads which cross the village and by walking its boundary on the Open Forest.

Fritham is a particularly striking example of a vaccary because over the centuries it has not been greatly expanded and so much of its original round shape survives. The shape of other vaccaries, such as at Canterton, have been hidden by more recent fields enclosed from the Forest. Parts of the vaccary at Burley Rails can be walked as they have been taken into the timber growing inclosures.

Folklore says that the Forest was created when the Norman Kings took control of England after their victory at the Battle of Hastings. With the Forest came the destruction of farms and villages and the introduction of new laws and terrible punishments.

Historians studying places like Fritham paint a different picture. Documents which have survived the centuries record that before and after the Norman conquest, the tenant of the vaccary kept producing cheese to pay the rent. Archaeologists have not discovered the remains of lost villages and abandoned farms which would support the folk tales of the destruction of villages. The Norman conquest may have been a catastrophe for the Saxon Kings and their noblemen, but to most ordinary people there was little change.

The Saxon name for land that we would now think of as the New Forest is *Ytene*. By 1079 the Norman Kings were calling the area *Nova Foresta* or New Forest. The name stuck and is still in use over nine hundred years later.

The fields at Fritham were first laid out over a thousand years ago.

Roydon Woods

South of Brockenhurst there are a series of paths linking the churches of St Nicholas at Brockenhurst to St John the Baptist at Boldre, and also linking the Filly Inn at Setley to the Red Lion at Boldre Bridge. These paths run through the Roydon Woods Nature Reserve.

Above: *A lane through Roydon Woods.*

Left: *Old plantations are being restored to heath in the nature reserve.*

The Church of St Nicholas at Brockenhurst.

The Lymington River at Roydon.

A Thousand Years of Worship

The Church of St Nicholas at Brockenhurst has been a place of worship for over a thousand years. A great yew tree grows by the church. This huge hollow tree has been studied by archaeologists and a certificate of the tree's age is on the church wall by the font. Among the ancient graves is a cemetery from the 1914–18 war, where men from New Zealand regiments are buried together with a solitary Indian.

The nature reserve at Roydon is a landscape of small fields, wood pastures, coppices, heaths and bogs running either side of the Lymington River. The nature reserve includes about 400ha of New Forest countryside which includes many of the same habitats and landscapes found in the Open Forest.

Roydon was once part of the Crown land but in the thirteenth century, the King gave it to Netley Abbey, a foundation on the far side of Southampton Water. After the dissolution of the monasteries nearly 500 years ago, the land was bought and sold many times. Realising the importance of the land for wildlife, the last private owner, Peter Barker-Mill made a gift of the estate to the Hampshire Wildlife Trust.

The landscape around the Roydon Woods has a special place in the history of landscape and nature conservation. This is because two of the most important people in countryside conservation in England found inspiration from this part of the Forest.

Boldre was the home of the Reverend William Gilpin from 1777–1804. Gilpin was inspired by the English landscape and was a popular author on what he described as 'picturesque' beauty. The ideas which Gilpin made popular were radical.

Rich travellers on their journeys overseas appreciated the landscapes and ruins of classical Greece and Rome. Gilpin's journeys took him around England and he saw the English countryside as containing places of beauty which previous generations had seen either as dangerous or just ordinary. Gilpin wrote that dramatic elements in the landscape such as rocks and gnarled ancient trees could inspire a sense of excitement and awe. The gentler landscapes of countryside could be sublime and be naturally arranged to be beautiful.

Memories of the *Hood*

William Gilpin was the vicar of the Church of St John the Baptist at Boldre from 1777–1804. The church contains memorials to those who lost their lives in the sinking of HMS *Hood* The ship was sunk with the loss of 1417 lives during the battle to sink the German battleship, the Bismark, in 1941.

St John the Baptist, Boldre.

Gilpin was so well known that other authors and artists would make fun of him. However, his ideas inspired garden designers such as 'Capability' Brown in creating the new landscape parks for the stately homes of England. His ideas were also taken up by poets and painters.

By 1810 it was possible for the poet William Wordsworth to be understood when in his guide to the Lake District he argued that such beautiful landscapes should be treated as 'a sort of national property, in which every man has a right and interest who has an eye to perceive and a heart to enjoy'. Wordsworth and Gilpin were at the very beginning of our appreciation of the beauty of our landscape, as well as the recognition of the responsibility which enjoyment brings to safeguard beautiful countryside for everyone.

Gilpin helped people learn about natural beauty. A hundred years after his death another writer lived at Roydon who helped popularise natural history and nature conservation. W. H. Hudson was born a Spanish-speaking Argentinean of an English

William Hudson came to England in 1874 at the age of thirty-three and made his living as an author and journalist. He arrived in England at Southampton in early May and seeing the shore of the Isle of Wight and the New Forest he wrote: 'It seemed so surpassingly lovely – so like a dream of some heavenly country'.

Below: Roydon in summer is a good place to see silver-washed fritillaries and other butterflies.

Hudson lived for most of the time in London. He travelled a lot, particularly in Wiltshire and Hampshire, and got to know the New Forest well. After several visits including a time living in Roydon Farm he published *Hampshire Days* in 1902. *Hampshire Days* celebrates the beauty of the Forest and Hudson's sense of wonder at its landscapes and wildlife.

Hudson's writing style appealed to a mass audience and his books and articles sold well. Like an early-twentieth-century Richard Attenborough, he was able to describe in words what we now see on natural history programmes on television. Like television, he reached a wide audience. Hudson was appalled by the destruction of natural beauty and told his readers about threats to nature from changes in farming, the spread of suburbs and the growing tourist industry. Hudson campaigned against the killing of wild birds for feathers to decorate hats. This campaign lead to the founding of the Society for the Protection of Birds, now Europe's biggest wildlife charity. Hudson was their chairman and a vigorous campaigner for wild nature.

Opposite: W. H. Hudson particularly loved the abundant birdlife around Roydon

Clockwise, starting top left: Hawfinches are a common sight around Roydon; spotted flycatchers enjoy the mixture of heaths, meadows and woods; nuthatches feed on nuts, seeds and insects and redstarts nest in the ancient trees.

He also applied the scientific observations of a naturalist with a moral belief in the responsibility that people have to care for nature. He felt that an understanding of our place in nature made us better, happier people. He was concerned about extinctions as he realised that all species depended on one another as 'links in a chain, and branches on the tree of life'. Hudson sought to protect nature by helping others to learn to love it. He also feared that the very richest landscapes could become tamed or cluttered by too many people. Hudson was one of the founders of nature conservation, not as a scientist, but as a spokesman for a popular movement in which everyone could take part.

Above: With a small farm ponies can be taken off the Forest and made ready to be sold.

Below: The house cows provide milk and butter.

There is no such thing as a typical commoner's holding. Each commoner is different in the way they find somewhere to live and put together enough land to care for livestock.

Among the footpaths between Frogham and Blissford is Ann Sevier's farm. The family have lived around Blissford since 1650, not moving more than 200 yards from the present farm. The Seviers trace their lives as commoners in the Forest back 13 generations.

The farm is small at 11 hectares and is divided into nine fields. There is a heavy annual job in maintaining the many hedges. The farm is a full-time commitment but only a part-time income.

The land is now all pasture but within living memory some of the small fields were cultivated. The fields include an impressive range of habitats, a bog in one hollow, a wooded stream and wild daffodils in another. There are as many wildflowers as there is grass in summer. In winter the land lays cold and wet.

The farm has been a dairy with milk straight from the cow delivered to local houses from the back of the van. The dairy is no longer commercial but there are three milking cows for the house with another three following. The calves are fattened and finished on the farm. They are slaughtered locally and the meat sold to friends and neighbours who appreciate the quality that comes from traditional farming. The holding supports about 20 ponies which run on the Open Forest for most of the year. Ponies needing attention, or being prepared to be sold, may be held in the fields over winter.

The Seviers are fortunate enough to own their farm having bought it in the 1930s after the Coventry estate was broken up. Many other commoners rent land if they can find it and the landlord has not abandoned farming altogether. The special quality of the Forest's landscape depends on future generations of commoners working farms like this.

BUILDINGS IN THE COUNTRYSIDE

With a population of over 34,000 there are a lot of homes in the National Park. The architecture of a Forest village has been politely described as 'unremarkable but inoffensive'. The building that has gone on in the Forest since the 1920s has created a legacy of houses of which few are particularly special.

There are some splendid buildings among the everyday designs of most Forest homes. It is the work of the rich which tends to have survived the longest. Until the coming of the railway and access to cheap bricks, most people would have lived in houses made out of the materials they could find locally. Cob, a mixture of clay and fibres was widely used. The trouble with cob is that unless you keep the walls and the roof dry it quickly turns back into mud. There are still cob cottages in the Forest but most have been extended and made comfortable with all modern conveniences. It is difficult to imagine from their well-appointed charm the lives of their previous inhabitants.

A cob cottage and barn at Woodgreen.

A twentieth-century equivalent of cob was the combination of creosoted boards and corrugated iron sheets. There are a number of sturdy agricultural buildings, and even the occasional home built with these inexpensive but readily available materials. These 'board and tin' buildings are becoming scarcer and those that are left are an important reminder of a rural way of life which was once widespread in the Forest even a generation ago.

Above: *Little Denny at Woodlands.*

Right: *The Tin Church at Bartley has been converted into the village hall.*

The Crown and the Church were wealthy and have left substantial buildings. Wealthiest of all were the religious foundations until King Henry VIII broke their power. There were two large religious houses in the Forest, at Beaulieu Abbey and Breamore Priory. Breamore Priory was established by Augustinians and compared to Beaulieu, was not particularly powerful or prosperous. The ruins of Saint Michael's Priory at Breamore have now disappeared into the meadows of the Avon.

The remains of Beaulieu Abbey are still impressive in their size and strength. The Abbey was founded in 1204 and for over 300 years it enjoyed great power and wealth. In 1538 King Henry closed down the Abbey, driving out the monks and demolishing the great Abbey Church and many of the monastery buildings. The main gatehouse to the Abbey was kept and turned into a fine house.

This is now the home of the Montagu family. The refectory of the Abbey was the hall where the monks would eat and listen to the Bible being read. After the Abbey Church was demolished the refectory was converted into the parish church. The tradition in Christian churches is that the main altar is placed at the eastern end of the church. As the refectory was originally built at right angles to the Abbey, the altar in this parish church is at the southern end.

The Abbey Church at Beaulieu.

The ruins of the Abbey can be seen around the parish church and among the grounds of what is now the National Motor Museum.

St Leonard's Grange, part of the farms of Beaulieu Abbey. A modest barn has been built within the ruins.

Relics of Recent Wars

The Forest's landscape has many reminders of recent conflicts. The flat plains and heaths of the Forest were ideal for constructing airfields in the Second World War. The concrete has been lifted but the footprints of the runways through the heaths are still clear at Ocknell, Holmsley and Beaulieu.

Ibsley airfield crossed over what is now the boundary of the National Park. The runways have been dug out as part of the gravel works which form Ibsley Water and Mockbeggar Lake. The memorial to the airmen, their chapel and other buildings all fall within the National Park but the remains of the control tower are just outside. The Spitfire squadrons of Ibsley airfield have been succeeded by the flocks of water birds of the Blashford Lakes Nature Reserve.

Above Ibsley on the heaths of Ashley Walk, the Air Ministry experimented with new bombs. High on the hill various targets were created in the heather including giant chalk crosses and armoured submarine pens. The bomb craters have healed over and the concrete and chalk have been colonised by wildlife. One of the chalk crosses is home to a colony of early gentian, a plant found in southern Britain but no where else in the world. When botanists search for this plant on Ashley Walk it is a case where quite literally 'X' marks the spot.

The Canadian Memorial.

The simple wooden cross on Mogshade Hill was erected by soldiers of the Canadian army in 1944. For a few months church services were held here while the armies gathered and waited for D-Day. All other signs of the camps in this part of the Forest have gone. The cross remains as a memorial to those who served, and veterans continue to care for the site and the cross is decorated with modest personal mementos.

On the other side of the Highland Water Inclosure from Mogshade is Millersford. In a glade by the road stands a cook-house fireplace and chimney, decorated with water-worn pebbles. This is the all that remains of a Portuguese army camp dating from the First World War. The camp was home to servicemen whose contribution to the war effort was managing the timber in the nearby inclosures. The camp has been cleared away but the fire-place was kept and restored by the Forestry Commission and the Portuguese Government.

Above: *The ruins of the control tower of Ibsley airfield.*

Left: *Looking out from the National Park across to Mockbeggar Lake, once Ibsley airfield.*

Below: *The Portuguese Fireplace.*

The railway meant that the Forest became easily accessible and a fashionable place to live from the mid-nineteenth century. The railway had taken a roundabout route through the Forest after lengthy negotiations between the railway company and the many Forest interests.

The Southampton to Dorchester line was opened in 1847 along a winding route nicknamed Castleman's Corkscrew or The Watersnake. Lyndhurst Road Station, now renamed Ashurst New Forest, had to be built many miles to the east of Lyndhurst village. The next station to the west, Beaulieu Road Station, stands in the open heath. This station was ideal for Victorian naturalists to walk off the train into wonderful countryside but remote from anywhere of consequence. As Beaulieu Road is surrounded by Open Forest, there were few development opportunities and the station remains a curious backwater on the mainline service between London and Bournemouth.

When the railway stations were built among the fields of enclosed countryside there was a building boom from Ashurst in the east to Sway in the west. Brockenhurst grew with new streets of brick villas of the new railway town which linked together the ancient manors of Brookley, Brockenhurst and Mapleham. Modern day Brockenhurst is mostly in the historic manor of Brookley.

Brockenhurst Station was the junction for a number of branch lines. Only the Lymington line survives today as it serves the Isle of Wight ferry. In the ticket office of Brockenhurst Station there are photographic portraits by Julia Margaret Cameron of the eminent Victorians who took the train and ferry to the Isle of Wight.

The great poet Alfred Lord Tennyson had made his home at Farringford under the High Down on the west Wight. Cameron, a near neighbour of Tennyson, convinced many of his visitors to pose for her. She had not only mastered the new technology of photography but also had an artist's eye for capturing the character of her sitter, and Tennyson is among the portraits at Brockenhurst Station. His portrait has been described as the picture of a mad monk.

There is also a portrait of Charles Darwin. This picture of an old man with a greying brow and a large intellectual forehead remains one of the strongest images we have of the genius whose thinking changed how we view our place in the world.

The wealthy Victorians and Edwardians built substantial homes throughout the Forest with many fine examples of Arts and Crafts design. Appletree Court, a private house that became the District Council's offices in Lyndhurst, is from this period. Most of the fine country houses of this period are still in private hands.

Chapel in the Fields

The Chapel of All Saints' at Thorney Hill near Bransgore stands alone in fields enclosed from the former Shirley Common. The chapel was commissioned by Lord Manners of the Avon Tyrell estate and built of concrete and aluminium between 1906 and 1908 to a classical design by Detmar Blow. The chapel is highly decorated with murals by Phoebe Traquair, one of the leading figures in the Scottish Arts and Crafts movement.

Appletree Court, the District Council's offices at Lyndhurst, was once a gentleman's residence.

All Saints' Chapel, Thorney Hill.

Unlike elsewhere in England, the Open Forest limited the ability of many of the Victorian towns to continue to grow. It was almost impossible to get permission to build on the Open Forest. Today when you approach Lyndhurst from Southampton you travel directly from the heaths and lawns of the Open Forest straight into the commercial High Street without passing through more modern suburbs. Smaller villages outside Lyndhurst such as Bank, Alum Green and Swan Green just stop where they meet the Open Forest.

Lyndhurst did not have a railway station but there was a good road into Southampton and access to the station at Ashurst. During the second half of the nineteenth century Lyndhurst was rebuilt and expanded. The Georgian church was replaced by the Victorian-Gothic-revival, coloured-brick, St Michael and All Angels. The church was designed by Sir George Gilbert Scott with stained glass by Burne-Jones and William Morris' company, together with a mural by Frederick Leighton. The new-found wealth of the Forest in the late nineteenth century is reflected in this gem of pre-Raphaelite art.

The Hargreaves family of the nearby country house of Cuffnells sponsored the development of the church. The modest Hargreaves family grave attracts visitors from all over the world. As a young girl Mrs Hargreaves, then Alice Liddell, was the inspiration for Lewis Carroll's extraordinary fantasies of *Alice in Wonderland* and *Alice through the Looking Glass*.

St Michael and All Angels beyond Bolton's Bench.

Rhinefield House

Rhinefield House, built in 1880–90 on the Saxon farmstead of *Sanhest* is now a country house hotel. The architecture has been described as a mixture of Elizabethan, Flamboyant and Gothic. The gardens of Rhinefield are one of the nationally important parks and gardens in the National Park.

Rhinefield House.

Classic callbox

The smallest listed building in the National Park is the telephone box in Beaulieu High Street. This 'K6' box was designed by Giles Gilbert Scott, grandson of George Gilbert Scott, who was the architect of the church in Lyndhurst.

Perhaps the most curious building in the National Park is Sway Tower. The 66-metre high concrete tower stands high above the heath and is visible as far north as Minstead. The tower was built by Judge Peterson between 1879 and 1885 using radical new building techniques inspired by spirit messages from the long-dead Sir Christopher Wren. Peterson was a spiritualist and one of a group of Victorians who believed the Forest was a place where pixies and fairies could be seen walking in the woods.

Above: *K6 telephone box, Beaulieu.*

Right: *Sway Tower from Widden Bottom.*

Another great champion of these notions was Sir Arthur Conan Doyle, popularly known for his Sherlock Holmes mysteries. Conan Doyle's final resting place is in the graveyard of All Saints at Minstead. His first grave was in Sussex where, in the spiritualist tradition he was buried standing up. His later reburial alongside his wife at Minstead was more conventional.

The grave of Sir Arthur Conan Doyle, Minstead.

Above: *The Trusty Servant and the village stocks on the green at Minstead.*

Right: *The Trusty Servant. A short name for a pub with a long explanation.*

Below: *Interior, All Saints' Church, Minstead.*

Minstead

Minstead is a village scattered along Forest lanes. At its heart is a village green with the church, a pub, and a shop.

The pub, the Trusty Servant records a four hundred year old job description.

All Saints' Church at Minstead survived the enthusiasm of Victorian 'restorers'. The church is arranged so that the local nobility had comfortable seats and could warm themselves by a fire. The musicians and the school children had separate seating in galleries above the congregation. Sermons could be preached from a pulpit with three heights, reflecting the seniority of whoever was giving the sermon.

A Trusty Servants portrait would you see
This Emblematic Figure well survey
The Porkers Snout not nice in diet shows
The Padlock shut no secrets he'll disclose
Patient the Ass his Masters wrath will bear
Swiftness in errand the Staggs feet declare
Loaded his Left hand apt to labour saith
The Vest his neatness Open hand his faith
Girt with his Sword his Shield upon his arm
himself and master he'll protect from harm

This 16th Century saying is believed to originate
from Winchester College in the days when pupils at
the college had personal servants possibly the first
recorded job description of staff required.

TWELVE

GOOD NEIGHBOURS
AND WELCOME GUESTS

The New Forest National Park was founded in 2005 and took up its full powers in April 2006. Apart from the slightly different Broads Authority, it was the first to be designated in England since the Northumberland National Park in 1956, and is is the latest layer in the crowded history of administrative change in the Forest.

National Park purposes

The National Park has twin purposes:

1 conserving and enhancing the Park's natural beauty, wildlife and cultural heritage and

2 promoting opportunities for the understanding and enjoyment of its special qualities by the public.

In pursuing these purposes, the National Park Authority must seek to foster the social and economic well-being of local communities.

A National Park is administered by a National Park Authority. The National Park Authority is a branch of local government and is made up of people chosen both from local councils and from the public. Their job is to lead the delivery of the National Park purposes. The authority is not alone in this responsibility as all government bodies, both local and national, share the challenge of making the National Park work.

The New Forest is also Britain's smallest National Park. At 57,000ha, it is slightly larger than the 47,000 ha of the cities from Portsmouth to Poole which have grown up

**NEW FOREST
NATIONAL PARK**

The London-Bournemouth main railway line crosses the National Park.

either side of it. The National Park is so small it does not include all of the homes and smallholdings of Forest commoners. The Park boundary is drawn so tightly there are even small areas of Open Forest outside the National Park. New Forest commoning is something which happens inside and outside the National Park, and the National Park boundary does not mark the boundary of the landscapes, wildlife and economy of the Forest.

A home in the Forest and well-paid job in the city is easy with a little commuting. The National Park has mainline railway stations and a convenient motorway junction off the M27. There are few places in the Forest less than twenty minutes drive from a major industrial area.

In contrast, the profits from farming and commoning are small, if there is a profit at all. Nearly all commoners of working age have a job as well as choosing to live the commoning way of life. House prices and land prices now mean it is very difficult for young commoners to start up on their own. The Forest is a real asset to the economy and many people profit from it in all sorts of ways. The financial rewards to the people who actually manage the landscape are insufficient to help them compete in the new economy of the Forest.

The cities between Poole and Portsmouth already have a population of 1.7 million which is set to grow further. In the first twenty years of the National Park, an additional 22,000 houses are planned to be built just outside its eastern boundary and another 23,000 to the west. The towns which share a boundary with the National Park are already home to over 140,000 people. The National Park is well connected with easy access to motorways, mainline railways and airports. It has been estimated that 15 million people live within ninety minutes of the Forest. In the past, the Forest has been protected by its isolation. That isolation is over.

The pressures that the Forest is already experiencing are likely to increase. The cities have brought wealth to the area and people naturally want to enjoy their leisure time. As the cities have grown, the choice of places to enjoy in the countryside has shrunk. The Forest has increasingly been seen by the neighbouring cities as a place for recreation.

The new growth around the borders of the National Park has been planned without an appreciation of what this will mean for the Park. There is a real danger that the only places left for recreation will be the most sensitive landscape and habitats. The National Park is not big enough or tough enough to be the only significant open space for the cities of the south coast.

Motorways and trunk roads also cross the National Park.

Above: *Walking the dog at Long Slade Bottom.*

Right: *The car park at Smugglers' Road, Burley.*

Opposite: *The Open Forest is popular for horse riding.*

The last major review of recreation in the Forest was in the 1960s. This review established the current pattern of recreation on the Open Forest. The damage that recreation was doing to the Open Forest was dealt with by making most of the area car free and then providing over 140 official car parks and 10 Forestry Commission campsites. Since the 1960s there have been minor changes in recreation facilities but the overall pattern remains the same.

It is currently estimated that up to 24 million visitors enjoy the Forest each year, three quarters of whom come from the neighbouring towns and cities. Some of the 1960s facilities are looking very worn and there are places where the Forest is clearly suffering from overuse. In the same way as town planning in the 1960s is being looked at again so it is time to reconsider planning for leisure in the Forest.

Recreation in the Forest's countryside and coast has grown dramatically over the last forty years. The sheltered coast of the western Solent has welcomed a fleet of leisure boats and has developed harbour towns and villages with marinas and thousands of moorings. Fine houses have been built along the eroding coast, and car parks have been made on beaches and marshes. As the coast changes either we will adapt to the change and allow nature to take its course, or else we will have an increasingly engineered and artificial coastline. Climate change and sea level rise will not allow decisions to be put off for long.

Within the countryside when farmland is sold it does not usually get bought by commoners and local farmers. Agricultural land prices in the New Forest can be eight times the national average. The soil is not particularly fertile and Forest agriculture is far from profitable.

Strict planning rules mean there is little hope in building a new house on a field. Land for leisure, particularly for keeping riding horses, is what keeps the prices high. Across the Forest, farming is in decline. If we want to conserve the landscape of the Forest we need to help find a future for those who currently manage the landscape. We also need to find ways to help the new generation of leisure landowners fit into the ways of the Forest.

The Forest has always changed and it will continue to change in the future. Over the years the daily decisions by all of us will add up to make a different Forest. The Forest is not isolated from the changes in society and the economy of southern England. Decisions made outside the Forest by people not thinking about the Forest are just as important as those made in the Forest for the Forest. Part of the job for the National Park is to guide these changes and decisions.

If the National Park works well then what is special in the Forest will not only survive but in time there should be more of it. Those of us who live in or visit the Forest have a particular responsibility. The National Park is there to help us understand and enjoy what makes the Forest special. By enjoying what makes the Forest different, we can then understand what we need to do to look after it.

The Forest needs good neighbours and welcome guests. The decisions we all make today will determine the Forest of the future. We will have the Forest that we deserve.

FIND OUT MORE

Every year there are events in the Forest that you can join in and be shown more of what makes the place special. The tourist information centres in and around the Forest have details of what's on. The Tourist Information centre in Lyndhurst is based in the New Forest Museum, Tel: 023 8028 2269

The Christopher Tower Library in the New Forest Museum in Lyndhurst holds an excellent collection of Forest books both for reference and for sale. For details of exhibitions at the museum and library opening hours telephone 023 8028 6158 or visit www.newforestmuseum.org.uk

For more detailed information on the National Park read:

Bowen, G. S. (2004) *The Reverend William Gilpin* St Barbe Museum and Art Gallery, Lymington

Briscoe Eyre, G. E. (1883) *The New Forest: Its Common Rights and Cottage Stock-Keepers* Reprinted in 2006 by the New Forest Ninth Centenary Trust, Lyndhurst

Goriup, P. (ed) (1999) *The New Forest Woodlands* Pisces Publications, Newbury

Langford, A. (1992) *The strange death of King William Rufus: A New Forest Mystery* Ensign Publishing, Southampton

Nield, S. (2005) *Forest Law and the Verderers of the New Forest* The New Forest Research and Publications Trust, Fordingbridge

Tippett, B. (2004) *W.H. Hudson in Hampshire* Hampshire County Council, Winchester

Tubbs, C. R. (1999) *The Ecology, Conservation and History of the Solent* Packard Publishing, Chichester

Tubbs, C. R. (2001) *The New Forest* New Forest Ninth Centenary Trust, Lyndhurst

Wise, J. R. (1863) *The New Forest, its history and scenery* Henry Southeran, London

There is always up to date information on what's happening in the Forest on the internet.

Useful websites are:

Access land in the Forest	www.openaccess.gov.uk
Countryside Education Trust	www.cet.org.uk
Forestry Commission	www.forestry.gov.uk
Hampshire Wildlife Trust	www.hwt.org.uk
National Trust	www.nationaltrust.org.uk
The New Forest Association	www.newforestassociation.com
New Forest Commoners' Defence Association	www.newforestcommoners.co.uk
New Forest National Park Authority	www.newforestnpa.gov.uk
The Verderers	www.verderers.org.uk